The
F

The CIA Makes Science Fiction Unexciting

* * *

Dark Deeds & Derring-Do
From 1950 to Today

series editor **Joe Biel**
illustrated by **Keith Rosson**

CIA Makes Science Fiction Unexciting
Dark Deeds & Derring-Do
From 1950 to Today

First Printing March 1, 2013
ISBN 978-1-62106-829-7
This is Microcosm #76148

Significant portions of the original articles were contributed by Gena Mason and Scotty Mylxine, particularly pages 62 to 89 and 120 to 158, respectively.

Illustrated by Keith Rosson except
Illustration on page 6 by Sarah Oleksyk
Edited by Lauren Hage
Designed by Joe Biel

Distributed by IPG and Turnaround, UK

Microcosm Publishing
636 SE 11th Ave.
Portland, OR 97214
www.microcosmpublishing.com

Twelve years ago I was milling about in the basement of a used bookstore in Minneapolis, savoring their selection on nefarious activities. I related to my compatriot about my interest in writing on the topics in front of me. The following year I released *The CIA Makes Science Fiction Unexciting* #1. It was assembled furiously to be printed in time for a tour booked in an equally hurried fashion.

Looking back, reading these books I had been amassing, I was quite perplexed by the volume of names and organizations that had maintained a high-level presence in our government across generations. I didn't understand how even as redacted documents were released to the public, they could maintain their position in government. I felt that I could at least connect these stories to a new audience—a younger one, who would be hearing these stories for the first time.

It was important for me, at that time, to write with some credibility and not go too deep into rabbit holes. The public perception when you write about things like undercover spies and secrets tends to be, "Look at what these crazy, wacko conspiracy theorists believe! How ridiculous." Now, over a decade later I think the most important addition was a little bit of humor. Does that make me more or less mature?

In many cases evidence was destroyed or classified to rot until people wouldn't be interested anymore. It's fun to do your own homework. You can find things more startling than these and people chasing down each and every rabbit hole as a result.

Each one of these cases could easily fill 800+ pages to talk about each of the players and events, what we know definitively, speculations, and what led up to them. This book is a way to give you just enough bait and hook to pique your interest. Because getting started is the hardest part. The original zines in these series are all out of print or about to be. So despite giving others advice to the contrary numerous times, each of the first five issues are here, re-written and reprinted in this collection.

Lorraine MOTEL

VACANCY

TH
SCIE

Chapter One:
The Assassination o

E CIA MAKES
ICE FICTION
UNEXCITING

artin Luther King Jr.

Martin Luther King, Jr: Civil Rights Leader

Now why on Earth would the FBI and CIA be so interested in undermining and discrediting Martin Luther King, and then later offering substantial assistance in at least covering up his murder? That's the kind of thing that gets a person into trouble.

King was a powerful leader and speaker that unified a formerly unfocused, yet large group of Americans. He spoke charismatically and articulated things that his followers had only previously understood without words. As he saw it, his struggles to unite and gain equality for the repressed African American population was intrinsically linked to opposing the Vietnam war and the class struggles of all Americans, even those who didn't happen to be Black. He organized peaceful marches to gain labor recognition for underprivileged workers. His nonviolent stance was dangerously effective in helping the image and intentions of his movement. It made his work difficult to discredit in the ways that other Black radicals had been.

But his stated opposition to the war in Vietnam was not taken lightly. In 1966, he referred to America as the "greatest purveyor of violence in the world today," comparing American practices in Vietnam to practices of Nazi Germans in World War II. His critics said that he should focus on one issue, like organizing the sanitation workers of Memphis, but he described it as, "the giant triplets of racism, materialism, and militarism."

To make matters worse for the powers that be, King was rumored to be planning a Presidential bid in 1968. He denied the rumors were true.

The FBI, J. Edgar Hoover in particular, had a pathological, almost malicious hate for King. King had demonstrated his ability to instigate massive direct action campaigns and his supposed Presidential candidacy would appeal to people who were opposed to the war. To Hoover, opposing the war was evidence that King was a communist, which carries a similar connotation to calling someone a terrorist today.

COINTELPRO

COINTELPRO is an abbreviation for the FBI's domestic "counterintelligence programs" to neutralize political dissidents, discredit, and undermine activist groups working domestically in the U.S. Although the FBI has used covert operations throughout its history, the formal activities of 1956-1971 broadly targeted radical political figures such as Martin Luther King and his followers. Since the FBI believed their aims were righteous, their plots had few bounds in these goals, and incorporated blackmail, threatening families, and politically discrediting people with the media.

The FBI had been wiretapping King for years and planting paid informants inside his organization to gather information. They referred to him as "Zorro," the Spanish word for fox or "The Fake Messiah." In 1968 the FBI increased the surveillance even further as President Johnson feared that King would drive him out of the White House. The FBI was happy to oblige. Bugs were planted at "all present and future addresses" of King under approval from Robert Kennedy. The justification was that he was perceived to be acting under communist influence or under allegiance to foreign communist states, even though these allegations never found any supporting evidence beyond his public opposition to the Vietnam War. Hoover interpreted this new permission to mean that the FBI could bug anywhere King spent the night for extensive amounts of time, such as hotel rooms, friends' houses, families' houses, and more. By 1968 the wiretaps violated the privacy rights of 5,000-6,000 people. Despite this broad level of surveillance, no substantial evidence was ever produced in support of these claims. Instead, King spoke out about how the FBI was doing its job to protect him and other blacks in the south. The FBI took that comment personally and a full scale espionage war was engaged.

Cartha DeLoach, the head of COINTELPRO in 1968, was trying to convince King to meet with him. But King's office was particularly busy at this time and DeLoach's calls were not returned. Being ignored tarnished the FBI's image of King even more than being berated and criticized. Cartha talked about "removing" King and called him "the fake messiah."

One of Hoover's favorite methods was blackmail and the best way for a group of conservative, old, white, religious men to embarrass or discredit someone was with charges of sexual promiscuity and adultery. Bugged tapes could be doctored or "improved" to make a stronger blackmail case. The FBI would blackmail King with the tapes and send him anonymous letters trying to persuade him to commit suicide. Letters to his wife included "improved" tapes of King in supposed sexual situations with other women and suggested that she should leave him.

COINTELPRO operatives discredited King by infiltrating Black movements and turning marches and protests violent. On

King's visit to Memphis on March 28, on a march in support of the sanitation strike, undercover police and FBI agents posed as members of a militant group called "The Invaders" and turned the peaceful march into violence. The police ignored the violence and property destruction until the march passed through, at which point they violently attacked the protestors.

The Assassination

On April 4, 1968 Martin Luther King Jr was planning to lead a make-up demonstration for the striking African American sanitation workers in Memphis, TN. He was staying in the Lorraine Motel on Mulberry St. in one of the city's seedier neighborhoods. Because the previous visit on March 28 had erupted in violence and looting, his image of nonviolent revolution was tarnished. A child had been killed by the police and 60 more were injured. He wanted to show that a peaceful march was possible and to demonstrate the effectiveness of nonviolence. Approaching 6 PM, he was about to enjoy a prime rib and soul food dinner with Samuel B. Kyles.

Just before 6 PM, King walked out onto the balcony of his hotel room to greet the people on the street. He was on the second floor overlooking the motel's courtyard. At 6:01 as King stood alone on the balcony, a single shot from a high-powered rifle tore into the right side of King's face, forcing him backwards.

An aide came forward and pointed to where he had thought the shot had come from Brewer's Boarding House across the courtyard. It was later suspected, for unrelated reasons, that this aide was one of the FBI's infiltrators.

Rev. Ralph Abernathy rushed out from the hotel room to King's side. Abernathy attempted to speak with King calmly:

"This is Ralph. This is Ralph. Don't be afraid."

But King was already unconscious; lying in an ever-widening pool of his own blood. Andrew Young rushed up from the parking lot to check King's pulse but really knew it was already over. Five minutes later he was speeding in an ambulance to St. Joseph's hospital. He was pronounced dead at 7:05.

James Earl Ray

James Earl Ray is a tragic character almost from birth. Most of his career was spent committing petty crimes like robbing illegal gambling rings and prostitution circles. Each time that he attacked a legitimate establishment he was caught. He escaped

from prison in 1967 by burying himself underneath hundreds of loaves of prison-baked bread in a departing delivery truck.

By 1968 he appeared to be attempting to get away from his life of crime with the plan to eventually leave the United States for good. Ray made his efforts to become a cultured man as well. He took two months of dance lessons in L.A. and then two months of bartending classes. This also strikes me as strange and contrary to the "lone nut" character that he was painted as in the media. Was he truly a social animal or just trying to become one?

Ultimately what paid the most and what he knew best was crime. And allegedly, shortly thereafter, Ray began gun running operations for a man that he referred to as "Raoul" or "Raul," a man he met hanging out in sailor bars. Ray said he was in legal trouble and seeking money and new identification. Raoul promised to fulfill those needs, according to Ray. Perhaps his greatest tragedy was the conditions under which he wrote his autobiography, *Who Killed Martin Luther King Jr?*, while in prison. For the sake of coercing a confession, Ray was kept under interrogation lights 24 hours per day. Between being unable to sleep and intensive interrogation sessions, Ray turned out to be a fine author, though I suspect his work underwent heavy edits.

Ray was eventually convicted of singlehandedly killing Martin Luther King Jr. without a trial. Ray claims Raoul directed him to purchase the 30.06 Remington Gamesmaster rifle in Birmingham, AL to "show to potential clients" that was later claimed to be the murder weapon that killed King. Ray had originally bought a less powerful rifle but had exchanged it at Raul's urging. Ray says the same man instructed him to be in Memphis on April 4, 1968 and purchase the "pale yellow" (or white) Mustang that he was driving that day.

Ray checked into the New Rebel Motel on April 3 but moved to Brewer's Boarding House on April 4th at Raul's urging. While parking the car on the 4th Ray noted a very similar white Mustang parked next to it. After checking in, Raoul sent Ray to run errands and when he returned about 5:00, Raoul asked him to leave again so he could meet alone with clients, suggesting that Ray go to a movie. Ray didn't know what to do and eventually went to fix the spare tire he had discovered was flat. After fixing the flat, upon returning to Brewer's, Ray found the area full of policeman and fled the city, as a wanted prison escapee who was transporting guns. According to Ray, he found out that King had been shot while listening to the radio on his way out of town and discovered—to his horror—that the police were looking for a white man in a white Mustang. So Ray headed for Atlanta, where he had left his belongings earlier that year. He abandoned the car in an Atlanta parking lot and took a bus to Detroit, where he took a train to Toronto and hoped to find a way to leave North America for good. Ray applied for a passport under the name "Ramon George Sneyd." On May 6 Ray flew to London. He attempted to join a renegade army unit that would send him to Nigeria. As he boarded a plane to Brussells he was arrested as an international suspect in the murder of Martin Luther King Jr. and was extradited to the U.S. under charges of conspiracy.

Raoul

Raoul was a person that Ray referred to repeatedly in relation to his life from '67-68. Since Raoul's identity was never confirmed to be any existing person, the investigative committee concluded that he was a convenient construct and explanation for Ray to justify his movements and decisions. Key witnesses hadn't seen them together at their alleged 12-15 meetings. But some witnesses did hear James Earl Ray talking about getting money from and meeting with his brother. The committee dismissed "Raoul" as Ray's way to protect his brother(s) but it could also mean that "brother" was his euphemism for Raoul, which was the explanation from Ray's brother Jerry.

One unanswered question is: Why would Ray return the rifle for a more powerful one, if not by Raul's suggestion? He used the excuse that since the rifle was for deer hunting that his "brother" needed a more powerful rifle because he was hunting in Michigan where the game was bigger. This shows that Ray either changed his mind or didn't know what he was shopping for. In his autobiography he appears unfamiliar with rifles and also mentions that Raoul was quite vague in the type of hunting rifle that was needed in this case.

There were several "Raoul-like" characters who were uncovered later. One was a man named Jules Ricco Kimble who went by "Roland" or "Rollie" and was operating out of the right neighborhood at the right time to have met Ray as is claimed. Kimble was discovered by a newspaper reporter, while combing the area for such a person. The reporter eventually tracked down Kimble's girlfriend and discovered that Rollie kept a trunk full of guns and carried a police band radio. Kimble frequently asked his girlfriend to translate police broadcasts. He often called the U.S. from her apartment and she had kept the bills, hoping to collect from him someday.

Police investigators following Kimble lost track of him on July 18th; the same day that Ray claims to have met up with Raoul. Kimble was in New Orleans at the same time that Ray claims to have received a payment from him. Kimble's FBI file shows that he met with the Grand Dragons of the Klu Klux Klan on July 18, 1967 and his wife had seen guns and explosives in the trunk of his car that day.

In 1989, Jules Kimble, while serving a double life sentence, was interviewed by BBC reporters. He readily told them that he knew Ray and had been involved in the conspiracy to kill King; he also added that he had told this to the FBI investigation committee. He said that Ray didn't pull the trigger and was only a patsy. Kimble said he was familiar with the assassination scenario and implicated an element of U.S. intelligence headquartered in a southern city. Kimble said his job was to navigate Ray from Atlanta to Montreal in '67 to meet with a CIA identities specialist.

When this was investigated with an ex-agent of the CIA, the agent affirmed that the identities specialist had been in Toronto at that time and seemed quite surprised that anyone could have known that. The specialist's name: Raoul Miora! Which poses the question: When Ray refers to "Raoul" is talking about Kimble or Miora? Is it a composite of the two characters?

Another particularly fishy character was a gun runner operating out of Houston at the time. He sold guns stolen from a military base through the Marcello crime syndicate. The guns were obtained by a black ops military unit who split the profits with a man named "Raul" to fund their activities. This Raul was located living in suburban New York throughout the 80s and 90s with his family. A photo of him was obtained and a photo spread was shown to various people who had known him or worked with him in the past, including Ray. Every one of them correctly and immediately identified the photo of Raul. Later Raul's daughter confirmed the identify of her father on tape, connecting it to the photo. She looked at the photo, commented that it was of her father, unknowing that many other people had identified that man as present at the scene of the crime and being involved in the assassination of Martin Luther King, Jr. The daughter talked about how their family was being "protected" by the federal government, a quite strange service for a retired auto worker with no apparent ties to the government.

Other people who identified the photo as "Raul" include Glenda Grabow, Raul's former mistress and gun running assistant, and Loyd Jowers, owner of Jim's Grill. Jowers claimed Raul had organized meetings inside the grill with him present where they talked about killing Martin Luther King, Jr. Betti and Bobbi Spates, waitresses at the grill, also identified Raul as being present. His identity was further confirmed when he had a 6 minute phone conversation with Glenda. Never being able to pronounce her name correctly, he called her "Olinda." How often have you had a 6 minute phone conversation wtih a stranger? The FBI and investigation committee chose not to pursue these facts.

Ray's Aliases

Criminals use aliases all the time. It's a helpful way for an escaped convict to protect their identity. But in the case of Mr. Ray the sheer level of incredible coincidences are hard to ignore. Eric Starvo Galt, Ramon George Sneyd, Paul Bridgeman, and John Willard, the aliases Ray used after 1967, were all Toronto residents from the same neighborhood living. But none of them knew each other. And they each bore a notable and curious resemblance to Ray. They were all of the approximate same height, weight, hair color, and appeared to be the same age as Ray. Some of them had scars on their faces like Ray. Ray had plastic surgery on his nose in 1967 making him look even more like Eric Galt. Ray changed his hairstyle to look like several of these men. How did he assemble documents on these people? Ray had never been to Toronto.

All of his previous aliases had been people he had known from prison, an old neighborhood, or his brothers' friends. When probed about how he obtained these aliases Ray changes his story frequently and acts as if he can't recall the details. Then there's the whole matter of Raoul Miora, the CIA identities specialist also coincidentally being in Toronto at the same time. Ray's behavior appears to be an attempt at protecting whoever fed him this information.

Using Galt's name as his primary alias had the added bonus of "unknowingly protecting" Ray from the INS while in the United States and Canada in 1967-68. Galt was a top-ranking military man with maximum security clearance. If Ray was stopped routinely for a petty crime or traffic stop he would be let go as soon as the cops looked at his file. He had classified information and would look too important to be hassled by traffic and street cops. The investigation committee referred to the aliases as "uncredible" and "almost" unbelievable coincidences, but let the issue drop.

Ray's Funding

Ray was burning through money fast and furiously in '67-'68. Martin Waldron is one investigator who described it as Ray's "trail of free spending". This has been a major focus of several investigators of the case because it is one fact that has remained unanswered and Ray's explanation appears to be the only plausible one. Ray goes so far as to quote the specific dates, places, and amounts that he was paid by Raoul along with the services performed and the denominations of the bills. The FBI claims that Ray robbed his hometown Alton Bank in Alton, IL but sources show that he was living in Toronto at that time. But if Ray did, good for him. It would have been his first successful bank robbery.

When Ray was living in Toronto just after the murder he claims he was visited by a "fat man" delivering an envelope. He paid his rent the same day and purchased a plane ticket to

England. Investigators naturally questioned if this was a co-conspirator in the case. But the man went to the police shortly afterwards saying that he was a stranger delivering a lost letter. Given the circumstances, Ray was horribly paranoid at this point, rarely leaving his room for anything. But when the envelope was delivered, he came forward eagerly instead of requesting to have it brought to him. It seems that Ray had run out of money and waited to purchase his plane ticket for 6 days after it became available; hardly the behavior of a fugitive in a hurry. When confronted, the man was very edgy and refused to testify for the FBI, fearing for his life. The "fat man" cited the reasons for his fear as people being killed who were witnesses in the Kennedy assassination.

The Police's Story

The police's story is remarkably similar to Ray's. Up until a point. According to the police, Ray arrived in Memphis the day before the shooting. He originally checked into the New Rebel Motel but moved the next day to Brewer's Boarding House using the alias John Willard. Ray rejected a room that had no view of the Lorraine Motel in favor of one that did. The furniture was rearranged; most likely to watch King from a window perch. Ray brought a newly purchased pair of binoculars.

Another resident of Brewer's, William Anschutz, claimed that the he found the bathroom occupied several times in the hours before the shooting. Another resident, Charles Stephens, told William that the new tenant, Mr. Willard (Ray) was using the bathroom. After the shot was fired, both Stephens and Anschutz claimed they ran into the hallway and saw a man running from the bathroom with a bundle. It is speculated that Ray fired the fatal shot from a situated perch in the bathtub.

A package was later found by police in the doorway of Canipe's; an amusement company next door to Brewer's Boarding House. It contained a 30.06 Remington Gamesmaster rifle that was boxed, binoculars, ammunition, Schlitz beer, some food, and a portable prison radio (with Ray's numbers on it). Witnesses say the man who dropped the bundle was neat and clean and wearing a dark suit. Other witnesses had claimed that Ray looked neat and clean compared to the locals and was wearing a dark brown suit that day.

The same witnesses saw a white Mustang pull away from the curb leaving skid marks. Ray describes his own car as "a very pale yellow."

An abandoned car was found that was registered to Eric S. Galt matching a description of a "white" Mustang that was seen fleeing the scene of the crime. Two witnesses claimed to have seen a calm, dark man fleeing from Brewer's Boarding House carrying a package.

Fingerprints on the rifle and scope were Ray's. The serial number on the rifle matched the one that Ray had bought in Birmingham, Alabama. Thus Ray was the suspect for the crime and the popular belief was that he acted alone.

Despite this, there was no proof that Ray had ever fired the rifle. And it doesn't appear that Ray had ever killed anyone prior to April 4, 1968. The bathtub seems like an awkward and clumsy place for a crappy shooter to trust himself to make a single fatal shot with a rifle he wasn't accustomed to using. Up until this point in his life, Ray made a living by robbing small timers in the black market.

The origin point and trajectory of the shot were not called into question or scrutinized. It would appear that it was easiest for the police to believe that the shot came from the bathroom window of Brewer's. When witnesses did question this presupposition, their testimonies were dismissed.

It turned out later that Ray's rifle was never sighted. When tested it fired 4 inches to the left and 3 inches below target, failing an accuracy test. The investigation committee changed these numbers in their report to be less substantial and ignored any significance. Being that far off target would ultimately mean the difference between hitting and missing a target; especially a vital area like the head, where King was shot. Further, the death slug in King did not match the bullets located in the bundle.

The Bundle

Another important question is why would Ray take precious time to put the rifle back in the box like it had never been used and wrap it in a bedspread with all of his belongings? Why dump it on the sidewalk and leave evidence behind when the Mustang was just a few feet away?

The bundle was the critical evidence for the police to link the crime to Ray. The FBI and inspection committee speculated that Ray might have dropped the bundle in a panic after seeing police officers at the scene. But the witnesses' observations don't support the FBI's assumptions and it appears possible that the dropped bundle might be a plant designed to implicate Ray. The witnesses each claim that the dark suited man who dropped the bundle was not fleeing in a panic; rather, he walked casually and appeared to have deliberately discarded the bundle at that spot, detouring on his trip to the car to drop the bundle in that location. Canipe, the owner of the business, was one of the witnesses and he described the man to be "chunky" and "dark skinned," neither of which could be said of Ray. Canipe also testified that the bundle (containing the rifle) was dropped 10 minutes before the shot was fired.

A Gunman in the bushes?

The police and FBI tend to disregard the testimony of anyone who insists that the shooter wasn't Ray or that the shot originated from anywhere other than the bathroom window at Brewer's.

Solomon Jones said that he saw a man with something white on his face and something under his arm flee from the bushes in the courtyard after the shot was fired. Harold Carter affirmed a similar statement, and said that he saw a similar man from his position sitting just in front of the bushes that evening. He described a man with a high necked white sweater and a rifle or shotgun flee the scene. Both men were intimidated by the police unless they were afraid to repeat these accounts.

A broadcast on the police radio described a car chase that seemed to have never taken place. It said the cars (including a white Mustang) were headed northeast while Ray headed South.

"6:36 60 at Jackman and Hollywood. Mobile unit. East on Summers, from Highland exceeding speed limit. Blue '66 Pontiac going over 75 mph. 3 white males in blue Pontiac. North on Jackson."

At 6:48 "White Mustang is shooting at Pontiac. Austin Peay. Approaching the road going into naval base."

An adequate explanation was never given for this broadcast. Police Chief Holloman said it was a teenager involved in a prank and seemed troubled by further probe questions.

"I don't recall if we ever found out who it was."

Other unexplained Mustang references occurred at 6:10, 6:12, 6:35, 6:48, and 6:53.

Two Mustangs

One explanation that might help to explain these reports is the two white mustangs that were at the crime scene. FBI interviews and press reports at the time confirmed this. Two cars of the same make, model, and color with such close timelines in the immediate vicinity of the crime scene arouses suspicion. Ray described his car as "pale yellow" but every witness describes both Mustangs as white. One Mustang was parked almost directly in front of Jim's Grill and the other was parked a few car lengths south, closer to Canipe's.

Four witnesses established that the car in front of Jim's was there from about 3:55 till 5:20. The car in front of Canipe's was spotted at about 4:30 and again after 5:00. Witnesses said they noticed a white, dark haired man sitting behind the wheel until a little before 5:20.

One car left the area before six. Two men who were walking past the corner of Main and Vance remember seeing a Mustang pass directly in front of them between 5:15 and 5:30. The second Mustang screeched away minutes after the bundle was dropped.

Ray's movements and his alleged movements indicate that the car in front of Jim's Grill was likely his. He checked into Brewer's at 3:30 and bought binoculars at 4:00. Thus the Mustang in front of Canipe's likely did not belong to Ray. It was not spotted until between 4:30 and 4:45. If Ray was the assassin why would he wait in the parked car for 30-45 minutes instead of going inside and setting up the kill? Whoever dropped the bundle in front of Canipe's also likely drove away in the Mustang parked in front of Canipe's. Because the witnesses indicate that the car in front of Jim's left the area between 5 and 5:30, Ray's story that he ran errands at Raoul's urging between 5 and 6 seems plausible.

Two dark suits

Compared to most people in the neighborhood, Ray was well-dressed. On April 4th and 5th a second well-dressed man was reported, wearing a dark suit in the same neighborhood. The investigation committee chose not to investigate.

The owner of Jim's Grill called the police on April 5th because a man eating breakfast in a dark suit seemed peculiar. The other occupants of the bar were very disturbed and stressed by the shooting but this man remained calm. He was also seen eating dinner in Jim's Grill the day before around 4 PM. Ray also had seen this man on April 4th and described him as acting strange. The police questioned him on April 5th and he claimed that he had hitchhiked all night on April 3 to arrive early in the morning on the 4th and to be staying at Helen Wynne's, another rooming house in the immediate area. He was released without being fingerprinted because he "didn't fit the available description," which is odd, because he appears to fit the description of the suspect in every way. He had blue eyes and brown hair and was neat and clean dressing in a dark suit. The man's wife later admitted a "resemblance" between her husband and Ray. He claims that he was at the rooming house from 2 until 5:30 when he went to make phone calls, but he was described in several people's testimonies as eating dinner at Jim's Grill at 4 PM. He claimed to be having dinner at 6 PM in a restaurant while King was shot. Perhaps he had a second dinner two hours later.

He claimed that he had come to Memphis as part of his plan to get to California but two days earlier he had been several hundred miles closer to his destination in Little Rock, AR. He explains that he came to Memphis looking for someone who needs a car delivered to California. Later, his story changed to say that he had come to Memphis to "sell some things". He didn't mention going to California anymore.

The FBI made independent investigators more interested in this man by deleting sections of their own documents on him, mostly pertaining to the scene of the crime and his military record.

The Aftermath and Investigation

In 1974 Russell Byers, a St Louis underworld figure, told an FBI informant that he had been offered $50,000 to kill King. He claimed that in '66 or '67 a drug dealer named John Kaufman asked him if he was interested in making a huge sum of money. That evening they went to the home of John Sutherland, a wealthy and conservative patent attorney. Sutherland was wearing the full dress of a Confederate colonel's uniform and was surrounded by Civil War memorabilia. He offered $50,000 for Byers to kill King or have him killed. Byers agreed to think it over but eventually forgot about it. To his knowledge nothing developed from that meeting.

Investigators later determined that Ray may have found out about the offer from Kaufman's friend, Hugh Maxey, his former prison doctor. Ray had served time with John Paul Spika, who is Byer's brother-in-law. Under pressure, Spika later said that he told Ray about the offer and was mysteriously killed shortly thereafter. Ray's sister owned the Grape Vine Tavern, a bar in St. Louis where underworld types hung out to make contacts. Ray's brother John was the manager. Ray could have learned of the offer there, particularly given that the George Wallace headquarters

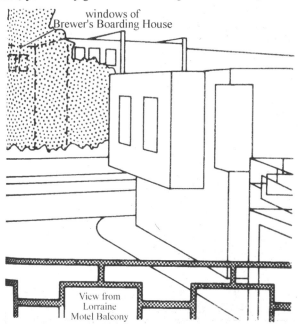

windows of
Brewer's Boarding House

View from
Lorraine
Motel Balcony

was across the street where Sutherland was a huge supporter. While there is no hard evidence to support this motive, the committee did research these details, found it plausible, and did seem to suggest conspiracy, by the very definition of "more than one person working towards a common goal."

The prosecution was able to successfully put Ray at the scene of the crime but could never prove that he was the shooter. They could prove that he had a palm print on the rifle but not that he had ever fired it. It was said that it was "possible" the 30.06 bullet found in King was fired from Ray's rifle but that it was also possible it was fired from any number of other, similar rifles that were in Memphis that day. In a legal setting guilt and conviction work on a system of no "reasonable doubt." Since the facts were never brought into question it was easy for the prosecution to walk all over Ray as his lawyer, Percy Foreman, failed to represent him; neglecting to challenge or object to any statements made against him.

Another unanswered question is: If Ray acted alone, how would he have known that Brewer's was connected to the adjacent building containing the bathroom where the shot supposedly originated? It was not visible from the street and he had not been inside the upstairs of Brewer's until the day of the shooting.

Ballistics

Many questions remain about the trajectory of the bullet involved because the scenario was never established. For some reason, the investigators never determined the position that King was in when he was shot. This would normally be important to determine the angle that the bullet traveled and trace it back to its source. Of course these same investigators seemed strangely and heavily invested in "proving" that the shot came from the bathroom window, going as far as quieting and discrediting witnesses who said otherwise.

Ray had always been a very poor shot and was aware of this. Why would he trust himself on the chances of one bullet at such a distance with so much brush obscuring his view? Was he aware that the rifle was not sighted and fired so far off its mark?

At the evidentiary hearing for Ray, a former FBI ballistics expert said that not even the most skilled gunman could have successfully pulled off the shot in the manner suggested by the prosecution. According to the expert, to effectively achieve such a shot, the butt of the rifle would have to be stuck six inches into the wall. The prosecution claimed that Ray had contorted himself into a position around the bathtub to approximate this. But as a crappy shot without experience, it smacks of the kind of luck that a failed criminal like Ray would never experience.

Ray's Lawyers

After being extradited from Britain on charges of conspiracy, Ray was confined for eight months in a cell bright enough to simulate daylight. The lights and guards were present 24 hours a day. Closed-circuit cameras and microphones monitored his every move.

Under these extreme conditions, as his physical and mental state deteriorated, Ray's attorney, Arthur Hanes, continually pressured him to plead guilty. Ray had been claiming he was a patsy in a larger conspiracy and continued to insist on a trial.

At the same time, William Bradford Huie was paying Hanes for information for a book he was writing on James Earl Ray. Huie suggested the money could pay for a trial. But as the clock ticked, Huie was casually leaking far too much of Ray's story to the press, and thus the prosecution. It was in Huie's best interest to produce a guilty plea from Ray, since his readers would be reading the information in his book that otherwise would have come out in the trial. This was not lost on Huie, who went as far as writing lies to market the book that the public accepted. Huie indicated that the palm prints in the bathroom and room #5 belonged to Ray, which they did not. This allowed the police to never reveal who these prints actually belonged to.

James Earl Ray's brother Jerry advised him to dump Hanes and contact Percy Foreman, a prominent criminal defense lawyer known for being aggressive. Ray was hesitant but other lawyers were turning down the case.

Foreman eventually took Ray's case with an even more adamant insistence about Ray pleading guilty than Hanes. After Foreman was paid $165,000 to defend Ray, he refused any course except a guilty plea. Despite a promise not to contact any authors until after the trial, Foreman also entered into a contract with Huie; forging Ray's name. Ray continued to insist on a trial and Foreman responded by threatening that he couldn't guarantee his best efforts as defense counsel. Foreman hadn't researched the case or interviewed Ray beyond his needs to sell details to Huie.

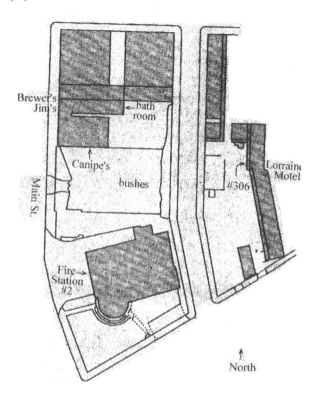

Brewer's
Jim's

← bath
room

Canipe's

bushes

#306

Lorraine
Motel

Main St.

Fire
Station
#2

↑
North

As the trial date approached, Ray feared the judge wouldn't allow new counsel yet again. Out of desperation and instead of letting Foreman throw the trial, Ray pled guilty as an act of desperation after being whittled down by his environment and the attitudes of his attorneys. Three days later Ray appealed the guilty plea.

But the process of appeals was equally stacked against Ray. While Judge Preston W. Battle was reviewing Ray's appeal request he died mysteriously of a heart attack in his office. Federal Judge William E. Miller also died of a mysterious heart attack while at the courthouse reviewing Ray's request for a trial. Both appeared to be giving Ray a chance at a fair trial. When the trial did finally happen, Forman objected to no questions from the prosecution, not even leading or improper ones. He performed no cross examination of witnesses.

The FBI's Involvement

At the scene of the crime, the FBI didn't radio in that King had been shot until 30 minutes after the shooting. There was no explanation of why they waited so long and this gave the shooter(s) the valuable time that was needed to escape.

Days before the assassination, the FBI had prepared a speech for Senator Robert Byrd to deliver to the Senate condemning King's actions. It alluded to King as a communist. The FBI planned to create its own "Black messiah" to replace King.

On King's previous visits to Memphis he stayed in the Holiday Inn, a white-owned and patronized hotel. A main agenda of the demonstration was a boycott of downtown white businesses. Cartha DeLoach, the head of Cointelpro, was involved in a campaign to embarrass King because of his decision to stay in the Holiday Inn, instead of a Black-owned and patronized hotel, like the Lorraine. Several articles were published labeling him as a hypocrite and influenced his decision to stay at the much more vulnerable Lorraine Motel for his next visit, unknowingly assisting his own murder. The day before the assassination, King was moved to a different room at the Lorraine. His final destination was in a much more vulnerable location than his secluded room on the second floor. When hotel employees were questioned about moving King's room, they reacted with fear and ignorance. The investigation committee dismissed these aspects, saying that Martin had always stayed in the Lorraine motel in room 306, but it was the first time he had stayed at that particular hotel and it was his only night in that room.

After King's assassination the FBI continued surveilling King's family and followers for another year. They planned to secretly publish a book as a hit piece on King's legacy along with newspaper stories undermining the King family. *Life Magazine* published a story about Ray as a "lone nut assassin" containing a considerable amount of factual inaccuracies about his childhood life and family and slapped a photo of his grade school class on the cover. The photo was centered on what appeared to be "the mean kid" while Ray was almost completely obscured behind someone else's head. The effort to promote Ray as the "lone nut assassin" was later revealed to be part of the FBI's written agenda.

Perhaps the most apparent ethical conflict became clear when the same intelligence detail of the FBI who was assigned to harass, threaten, and try to convince King to kill himself were then assigned to investigate his murder. They simply did not seek the truth in their investigation. One FBI supervisor was elated when he found out King had been shot and was literally jumping for joy when King was pronounced dead. He was assigned on the detail to investigate the assassination.

"The feeling against King was so strong that if the FBI had had advanced information of an assassination plot against King and no one else knew about it—they would sit on it." said Arthur Murtaugh, a former agent. He doesn't believe the FBI ever investigated the murder. Within 24 hours of the assassination, the FBI issued a statement that no conspiracy was involved, but that didn't prevent them from extraditing Ray from England on charges of conspiracy.

It took the FBI and local authorities 14 days to discover that Eric Starvo Galt was actually James Earl Ray despite the fact that Ray's prison radio—bearing his inmate numbers—was left at the scene, identifying him immediately with any inspection. Galt was also the name that Ray had used when identifying himself to Raoul.

Randolph Erwin Rosenson was a government informer known as "Randy Rosen." Most FBI files pertaining to him are completely classified but the remaining portions show that he paralleled Ray's movements in 1967-68 including Ray's trip to Birmingham where the supposed murder weapon was purchased.

A local reporter in Memphis, after reviewing photographs of the crime scene, discovered that there was not a clear view from the bathroom window to the balcony of the Lorraine. The view was completely obscured by branches from 10-12' foot oak and willow trees and overgrown brush in the courtyard. As this revelation was being discovered the city made a decision to cut down all of the trees. The public works director testified that he was woken up on the morning after the assassination and ordered to cut the brush to the ground immediately and to trim back all of the trees. Is it worth mentioning that tampering with evidence in a crime scene like this is obviously illegal?

Years later, when the Senate was debunking the Warren Commission reports, it became questionable whether or not the FBI's investigation of King's assassination was credible. The Senate discovered that the FBI had destroyed evidence, suborned perjury, and committed perjury in order to protect the killer(s) of John Kennedy.

Frank Holloman

Frank Holloman was the chief of police and chief of the fire department in Memphis in 1968. Previously, he worked as an FBI agent for 25 years in offices that monitored King in Atlanta, Memphis, and Jackson, Mississippi. He bugged King in Memphis when the sanitation strike was developing and was a close, personal friend of J. Edgar Hoover. In the hours before the assassination, Holloman pulled all African American police and firemen from the scene of the crime and positioned them elsewhere with no logic and little explanation.

Floyd Newsum

Floyd Newsum was a fire fighter and avid King follower at Station 2 during April of 1968. The day of the assassination he was moved out of the area to Station 31. A reassignment like this is typical if one station is overstaffed while another is short staffed, but this case was quite the opposite. Newsum's relocation made the equipment at station 2 inoperable due to short staffing and he was an extra, unnecessary man at Station 31. The official reason cited for the move was that it was for his protection. Protecting him from what? Station 2 has a clear view of the Lorraine motel and was used as a post for the police and FBI to monitor King.

In an interview he responded, "There is no way that they could have thought that they were doing me a favor, protecting me, or making me more comfortable by transferring me. I am sure that I was not moved because of considerations of my safety."

If Newsum had been outside the fire station during the shooting he would have seen the killer flee with only a few yards between them.

Another African American positioned at Station 2 that day was moved to Station 33.

Ed Redditt

Ed Redditt was the brains behind the Memphis police department's security detail on King. But on the day of the murder his security detail was reduced from ten people down to two. When King arrived his handlers requested not to be shadowed by security and the police chief was eager to dismiss the security detail entirely. Given the way that King had been treated in the past, it was common for King and his followers to have distrust for the police and their work. Redditt insisted on keeping a two man security team after he was told to go home the first time.

Two hours before the shooting Ed Redditt got sent back to HQ. There he was told about a contract on his life and he was immediately sent to a hotel. Supposedly a secret service officer flew to Memphis to share the information and the heads of every law enforcement operation in the region were present for this meeting. Why didn't the officer simply telephone the information to the local precinct? Redditt resisted the order, insisting that his mother-in-law was very sick and he did not want to move her. Reddit assumed that he would be well enough protected at his post in the firehouse but was eventually forced to go home and told that there was "nothing to discuss." Other officers were sent home with him with the explanation that they were present to protect him.

Once they arrived at his home it became apparent that the officers were sent there to watch him, not to protect him. They insisted on being at his side at all times. They all sat in a car outside of his house as King was shot. Redditt was afraid to go inside because he thought the presence of the other officers would disturb his mother-in-law. When they heard that King had been shot, his mother-in-law was screaming "Dr. King Dr. King Dr. King, God take me instead of Dr. King" and the next day she died of grief.

The secret service knew nothing of a threat against Redditt. Their security detail's plan, which Redditt's partner, Richmond, did not carry out, was to go to the street and scout out the area, watching for people fleeing while the other radioed to the mobile unit. Instead Richmond did nothing and refuses to talk about it.

Witnesses

John McFerren, an employee of Liberto Produce, heard his boss, Frank Liberto, on the phone an hour before the shot saying "I told you not to call me here. Shoot the son of a bitch when he comes on the balcony," and that the person could collect $5,000 payment from Liberto's brother in New Orleans. When Frank Holloman and the FBI investigated they said it was unrelated to the King assassination "if McFerren had heard it at all." Why would a witness come forward with that story if he hadn't heard it?

Frank Holt, a truck unloader, heard Liberto say "King is a trouble maker and should be killed. If he is killed he will cause no more trouble."

Charles Stephens was the star witness of the prosecution. He had claimed to see Ray fleeing from the scene of the crime but

could not identify Ray. He was rewarded with $30,000 by the FBI to say that he saw Ray fleeing the scene, but couldn't seem to get his story straight. Before Stephens had received the bribe he gave descriptions that didn't fit Ray and admitted he did not get a good look at the man. The photos that he saw of Ray were before he had received plastic surgery on his nose. Stephens had supposedly identified Ray from seeing his profile and the surgery significantly changed his appearance from this perspective.

James McGraw, a cab driver, came to pick up Mr. Stephens approximately 3 minutes before the shooting and said that he was so drunk that he was unable to stand. Eventually, after getting frustrated, he left Mr. Stephens lying on the bed and left the building. He said that he also noticed that there were two white Mustangs parked in front of Brewer's and that the bathroom door was wide open just minutes before the shot was fired.

Loyd Jowers agreed that Mr. Stephens was noticeably drunk on April 4 and had been unable to pay his rent.

Grace Stephens, Charles' wife, had been in the room with him during the shooting and claims that Stephen never saw the shooter flee and was not able to leave the bed. She says that he was not wearing his glasses and is virtually blind without them. She was sober and claims to be the only one who had seen the person fleeing from the bathroom and that it was not Ray. She stuck by her story despite police and FBI intimidation and as a result was later committed to a mental institution for 20 years with no history of mental disorders. The doctors said she did not belong there and that her condition was worsening from living there. She was the only resident not granted visitors and 20 years later was released after pressure from independent investigators of the King case. Despite 20 years and a fair share of intimidation tactics, her story has never changed. Mr. Stephens eventually recanted his entire story. Their friends admitted they were afraid to testify after seeing what happened to the Stephens.

William Reed and Ray Hendrix observed Ray's Mustang at length and then watched Ray drive by them just before the shot. They noted that Ray had Alabama plates while the other Mustang had Arkansas plates. Their testimony was stricken from the investigation.

Paul "Buddy" was a taxi driver present at the time of the shot. He saw a man flee from the crime scene, scale down a wall, and enter a Memphis police cruiser. He reported what he saw to the police and was found dead mysteriously later that night. His employment history was removed from the cab company's files.

Betty Spates, a waitress at Jim's Grill, claimed she saw her boss, Loyd Jowers, run inside the back door carrying a rifle immediately after the shot was fired. She said that his knees were soggy and muddy like he had been lying in the grass.

The next morning Jowers told Bobbi, Betty's sister, that he had found a rifle behind the grill & was going to turn it in to the police. James McGraw collaborated her story, saying that Jowers had shown him the rifle behind the counter the next morning. If the rifle had been "out back" as he indicated, why hadn't the police found it? After McGraw passed away, his longtime roommate told McGraw's story under oath with a new ending—McGraw had thrown the rifle in the Mississippi River at Jowers' instruction.

Was the CIA involved?

The CIA did a good job of projecting the image that they had little interest in King. They kept a very small domestic file on his activities and received information mostly from the FBI. This illusion was destroyed when an agent revealed that the CIA was keeping their true files on King in the highly classified "Western Hemisphere desk" where it filed its anti-Castro operations. This type of secrecy alleges that those documents were politically sensitive, if not illegal. Documents released under Freedom of Information later revealed that the CIA was actually passing information on King to the FBI.

Like the FBI, the CIA was probably interested in King because of the supposed connection between "Black power movements" and communists. As a result the CIA infiltrated many groups and took photographs and monitoring militancy in black youths.

Kimble implicates the CIA in his statements saying they had seven operatives, including two snipers with identical rifles to Ray's. The operatives obtained police uniforms and two of them hid in the bushes. This may explain the person seen fleeing wearing a high-necked white sweater and carrying a rifle. If the primary shot failed, the other was to act as a backup. The rifles were deposited behind the boarding house and obtained by other operatives who resembled police officers.

Kimble's credibility is, of course, in question but his stories check out and align themselves with other facts of the case, including the CIA identities specialist that Kimble knew was in Toronto at the same time as Ray, explaining the sources of Ray's incredible collection of aliases.

Why Was The Military Present?

Information and testimonies provided many years later indicate the presence of at least ten military personnel at the scene of the crime for no apparent reason. Several witnesses came forward to testify under the protection of being anonymous. Two of them were members of a military sniper team, Alpha 184, an 8 man unit deployed to Memphis. From their testimony, it appears they are still a bit uncertain what actually happened. They had two pairs of men situated in vantage positions, targeting King. Their instructions were to shoot him in the body cavity once they received the order. They were told they were present to stifle the situation in the event of a riot and to kill King and Andrew Young to diffuse the situation, but this sounds like it would incense, not calm, a riot.

The teams had their scopes trained on King when he was shot and each thought that the other had "jumped the gun," firing the shot before receiving the order. Their commander referred to their mission as a failure and refused to talk about it later. Second hand sources informed them later that the shot was carried out by a civilian. Their teams went through desensitizing training before that day and were taught that King was a threat to democracy and an enemy of the United States. JD Hill was a member of this team and was extensively trained to assassinate someone in Memphis on April 4, 1968. He was under the impression that the target was going to be Arab. He was a top ranking special forces officer who was later mysteriously killed by his wife with a large caliber pistol. But how is a man with the skills and training of James Bond able to be murdered by his wife, a novice shooter barely over 100 pounds?

In addition to the sniper team there was an army photography unit on top of Fire Station #2. They gained access to the roof from the head of the station and took photos of King being shot and the shooter lowering the rifle in the bushes. These events are denied by their commanders and the official files.

Conclusion

In 1997, King's son Dexter met with Ray to express that their family believes he was innocent. Ray hired Jack Kershaw as an attorney who successfully met with representatives of the U.S. House Select Committee on Assassinations, who ran ballistics tests to show that Ray had not fired the fatal shot. The tests were ultimately inconclusive. After escaping from prison again in 1977, James Earl Ray died back in prison in 1998 from kidney disease and liver failure. William Pepper conducted a mock trial of the assassination for television.

As a result, in 1999 Janet Reno opened a new investigation into the assassination. A full 30 years after the assassination, William Pepper, successfully filed a wrongful death civil suit for the King family. The resulting civil trial concluded that Loyd Jowers was 30% responsible for a conspiracy to assassinate Martin Luther King Jr. Jowers was forced to pay $100 in restitution for the "wrongful death," an amount that could decidedly show fault without appearing that the family was seeking financial gain.

The court concluded there was an extensive conspiracy to kill Dr. King, including agencies of local, state, and federal

governments that constituted the remaining 70% of the responsibility. Most disturbing of all, only two reporters showed up to the press conference to discuss this development and news coverage of the trial was minimal, mostly on local networks in Tennessee, despite the unprecedented move to prosecute groups like the CIA and FBI. Other networks referred to the case as "old news" and ignored the trial's findings altogether.

The court ruled that Loyd Jowers was approached by Frank Liberto to be a middle man for delivering money and a package to repay an old debt. Jowers was privy to meetings in Jim's Grill, where he watched police officers outlining a scenario with Raul. One of which was Earl Clark, a well-known police sharp shooter. Jowers received a produce crate full of cash to be delivered to Raul. He waited in the brush with the shooter and then retreated into the back door of the grill with the murder weapon, where he was seen by Betti Spates, while the shooter fled to an MPD cruiser. Police were kept at bay and witnesses were threatened or killed. Cooperation was granted from nearly all branches of government. Jowers had the rifle disposed of shortly afterwards where it rests buried in the silt of the Mississippi River.

Ray appears to have been the ideal patsy; powerless to fight against organizations as powerful as these.

Aside from the FBI's corruption in the handling of the investigation of this case, many loose ends left unexplored, and an obvious perspective and agenda affecting the investigation, the most chilling part of it is that even after the civil court found them guilty, there was no way to pursue the next step, to prosecute the secret agencies of government.

If the CIA, FBI, COINTELPRO, and their brethren exist to protect the safety and best interests of the American people, then shouldn't these organizations be accountable to us, the American public?

Sources / Recommended Reading:

Philip Melanson *Who Killed Martin Luther King?* (Odonian, Berkeley, 1993)

William Pepper *An Act of State* (Verso, New York, 2003)

James Earl Ray *Who Killed Martin Luther King?* (National, Bethesda, 1992)

Mark Lane and Dick Gregory *Murder in Memphis: The FBI and the Assassination of Martin Luther King* (Thunder's Mouth, New York, 1993)

Harold Weisburg *Martin Luther King: The Assassination* (Graf, New York, 1971)

Chapter
Two

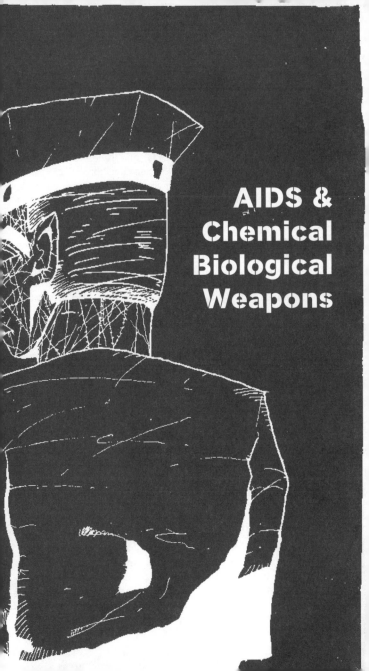

**AIDS &
Chemical
Biological
Weapons**

What is AIDS?

Acquired Immune Deficiency Syndrome (AIDS) is characterized by a gradual breakdown of the immune system, followed by opportunistic infections, general deterioration, and eventual death. The Center for Disease Control (CDC) sometimes defines it as a combination of 29 familiar diseases and conditions, including yeast infection, herpes, diarrhea, cancer, uncommon strains of pneumonia, salmonella, and tuberculosis. These symptoms are defined as AIDS when they appear along with protective disease fighting proteins or antibodies thought to be associated with HIV. HIV (Human Immunodeficiency Virus) is understood in science to be the virus that causes AIDS. The presence of HIV in the body is identified by concentrations of the proteins p24, p17, gp41, gp120, etc.

Socially, AIDS spread uniquely in five major cities in the U.S.: New York, San Francisco, Los Angeles, Chicago, and St. Louis. It was discovered in the early '80s and promoted as being 100% fatal. Initially hospitals and health care professionals were quite resistant to treating AIDS patients, largely due to misinformation about its transmission. As a result, cures and medications took years to develop and funding was difficult to obtain and funding streams were often corrupt.

Especially in the initial findings and for many years to come, AIDS primarily infected people who were also socially rejected in U.S. society; queers, blacks, prisoners, people living in third world Africa, and injection drug users. It is virtually unique for an epidemic of this nature to be confined to people of color or sexual orientation.

The Reagan administration tried to close down the CDCs lab that was researching solutions to AIDS until visible protests from the queer activist organization ACT UP made it impossible for them to continue ignoring the issue. In 1983 Luc Montagnier, MD was the doctor who first theorized that HIV was the cause of AIDS but hadn't developed the full proof. Robert Gallo, MD, building upon research that had been conducted in France, published reports concluding that HIV was the cause of AIDS.

In January, 1993 the CDC broadened the definition of AIDS to include people with lower than 200 T-Cells (a class of lymphocytes that work for the body's immune system) per unit of blood. This expanded definition caused the number of AIDS cases in America to double.

But by 2008 the epidemic had subsided and cases had reduced by over 90% in risk groups. *The Independent* ran a story that proclaimed "Threat of world AIDS pandemic among heterosexuals is over, report admits." Also in 2008, the *Washington Post* ran an article noting scientists continued surprise about how little they still understood about HIV's biology.

The origins and discovery of HIV and AIDS

French scientists at Pasteur Institute theorized that the HIV virus was a cause of AIDS in 1984. Shortly thereafter, Robert Gallo, director of America's National Institute of Health developed this theory and a blood test to detect the volume and type of antibodies. He delivered these findings to the CIA and U.N.

While on a quest to link HIV and AIDS, Hilary Koprowski and Robert Gallo discovered green monkeys in Africa had Simian Immunodeficiency Virus (SIV)—a virus that shares 40% of its genetic code with HIV. Gallo had developed an HIV test that would earn him millions of dollars in royalties if he could successfully link HIV testing to AIDS. His team developed the "green monkey theory," which stated that somehow the disease had jumped species from green monkeys to humans in Africa while simultaneously mutating. The implication was that someone had sex with a green monkey.

Through quite a few dubious assumptions and corruptions in funding streams, the theory seemed to rely on the inherent racism and stereotypes that Africans were so sex-starved that the theory could be sold as believable that someone would have sex with a monkey as the virus was significantly mutating. Because Gallo reported his "discovery" to the press before submitting to scientific journals, the theory did not undergo the usual peer review process of the scientific method. It was accepted as a scientific theory, allowing Gallo to sell his test and earn his millions.

The scientific method is typically used to test a theory as well as establish an ethical standard for establishing the validity of a hypothesis, which typically allows colleagues to dispute the claims published in scientific journals and poke holes in theories until they are proven or disproven.

Even in Gallo's own research, over 50% of the AIDS patients tested did not test positive for HIV and most contained antibodies that would provide immunity from infection, resulting in the scientific community's still limited knowledge pool about the way the virus behaves. Regardless, Gallo's theory was accepted and able to write history. He owned the patent on HIV testing because he had the opportunity to do so first, based on his "discovery" and conclusions. Gallo was later investigated for fraud in other scientific works.

This was new territory for science, as a retrovirus like HIV had never been known to cause a fatal disease before.

Additionally, AIDS does not behave like other infectious diseases; different AIDS risk groups have different symptoms. Most diseases are predictable and have specific symptoms. While AIDS affects males 85% of the time (affecting queer males 54% of the time), other diseases and viruses appear at random between genders. AIDS does not spread among healthcare workers like other diseases. And unlike most other diseases, AIDS has been in steady decline even among risk groups since 1993.

A History of Chemical Biological Weapons

1346—Mongols laid siege to Kaffa, a walled city on the Crimean coast. Diseased cadavers were catapulted into the city to spread what later would become the "Black Death"—a plague killing over 25% of the population of Europe.

1763—Allegheny Mountains' European colonists give friendly Natives smallpox infected blankets, killing many.

1830—The U.S. Army repeats the above act against the Cherokee Nation, in the infamous "Trail of Tears" massacre.

1877—Anthrax first cultured by bacteriologist Robert Koch.

1914-1918—WWI includes development and use of chemical weapons, particularly by U.S. troops. Over 1.5 million people injured or killed by chlorine or "Mustard" gas.

1932—U.S. Public Health Services tested 400 black men in rural Alabama infected with syphilis, doing experiments on its effects when left untreated. The men were not informed of their condition or that they were contagious. When penicillin became the standard treatment it was withheld from them and healthcare workers forbade the men from outside help.

A federal health worker blew the whistle and stopped the experiment. (*Tuskegee Syphillis Study, 1932-1972, Stephen Thomas and Sandra Quinn*)

1937—Nazi scientist Dr. Gerhard Schrader discovers "nerve gas."

1939-1945—WWII; U.S. military uses anti-crop agents against Germany and Japan causing widespread starvation. Dr. Joseph Mengele (an early pioneer in genetic engineering) conducts genetic experiments on prisoners at Auschwitz concentration camp. In Block 10 prison lab, Mengele maims victims for life with experiments on sexual organs, amputations, and finds out how long it takes people to die when pieces of their bodies are cut off. Japanese Unit 731 (under the leadership of General Ishsi Shiro) deliberately infects prisoners of war with a vast array of diseases in order to study the effects from an Army Chemical Biological Weapons (CBW) center.

1958—An international investigation commission of the Korean War exposes a multitude of germ weapons used by the U.S. against the Democratic People's Republic of (North) Korea. Three North Americans (John W. Powell, Sylvia Powell, and Julian Schuman) published germ warfare charges in the *China Monthly Review*. The Eisenhower Administration passed sedition charges but they failed to get convictions.

1960s—Mind-altering drug tests and aversion therapy, including electroshock, are used on California prisoners in Vacaville and Atascadero. Some tests are directed towards homosexual inmates, attempting to "convert" them. The World Health Organization (WHO) still classified homosexuality as a mental illness.

1961—First democratically elected Prime Minister of what is now The Congo and anti-imperialist, Patrice Lumumba was assassinated by CIA trained mercenaries (after subsequent attempts of murder by poison failed). CIA puppet regime led by Joseph Mobutu installed. Note: The Congo has some of the world's richest mineral deposits and along with Uganda later became the epicenter of Ebola and AIDS in Africa.

1961-1973—In the war against Vietnam, U.S. Chemical Biological Weapons (CBW) reaches its zenith in the most massive chemical war in history. Seeking to destroy crops, the U.S. aerially sprays 55 million kilograms of defoliants (mostly Agent Orange) on Southeast Asia. As a result, millions are poisoned, many develop cancer and die, and the next generation suffers horrendous rates of birth defects.

1966-1977—100 million blacks injected with smallpox vaccine in Central Africa by the World Health Organization.

1968—Porton Down and Fort Detrick collaborate in the successful transfer of genes between different strains of plague bacillus. The research was done "for purely defensive purposes."

1969, June—Stonewall Riots erupt in New York City, providing the catalyst for modern day Gay/Lesbian civil rights movement.

July—U.S. Department of Defense Appropriations for 1969-1970 called for $10 million for the creation of a killer virus with the clinical description of AIDS. Funding was approved. By this point, 100 men were dead as a result of the ongoing Tuskegee Syphilis Experiment.

1971—Pres. Richard Nixon counted on the conversion of military facilities (from abroad) to meet "pressing domestic challenges" (*NY Times* 10/19/71)

1971—CIA infected Cuban pigs with African Swine Fever. 500,000 pigs were slaughtered. (*Newsday* 10/19/71)

1972—Richard Nixon and Henry Kissinger coordinated efforts to turn Fort Detrick, a top biological warfare center, over to allegedly civilian National Cancer Institute (NCI) for cancer research. The NCI then turns the facility over to a civilian contractor Litton Bionetics, a major U.S. defense contractor with strong links to Intelligence.

1972—The World Health Organization published the following proposal: "An attempt should be made to ascertain whether viruses can in fact exert selective effects on immune function, e.g., by...affecting T-cell function as opposed to B-cell function. The possibility should also be looked into that the immune response to the virus itself may be impaired if the infecting virus damages more or less selectively the cells responding to the viral antigen." (A clinical description of the function of the AIDS virus.) —*Bulletin of the WHO*, vol. 47, pg. 257-274

1972—Tuskegee Experiment exposed; nationwide condemnation forced the government to end the project. The federal office who supervised the study was the predecessor of the Centers for Disease Control (CDC) unit in charge of the government AIDS program. The CDC, a journalist wrote in 1972, "Sees the poor, the black, the illiterate and the defenseless in American society as a vast experimental resource for the government."

1973—"Biohazards in Biological Research" conference held in Northern California; focused on discussion of the dangers of cancer virus research and what would happen if genetically engineered viruses escaped from labs.

1978, Nov.—Government sponsored NYC Hepatitis B vaccine study began on gay men at the NYC Blood Bank in Manhattan.

November—Dan White assassinates Harvey Milk, the most prominent gay activist of the century. Would the outspoken Milk have effectively challenged the official gov't lines on AIDS? Researcher Mae Brussell connects White's behavior to CIA/mind control connections.

November—Jonestown Massacre; 900 mostly black North Americans "suicided" (see John Judge's article, *"The Black Hole of Guyana"* in *"Secret and Suppressed"* for developing CIA/CBW connections)

1979—Three months after first Manhattan Hep-B vaccine, the first case of as-yet-unidentified AIDS appears in New York City.

1980—Los Angeles and San Francisco Hepatits-B vaccine trials begin.

1980—First West coast AIDS cases are recognized months later.

1981—Thousands of Haitians escaping the brutal repression of U.S.-backed Duvalier regime arrived on boats seeking refuge. Many refugees detained in detention centers for up to two years. Within months of incarceration at two of the centers in Miami and Puerto Rico, male refugees report a condition called Gynecomasia, in which they develop full female breasts.

1981—AIDS epidemic becomes "official," initially called GRID (Gay Related Immune Deficiency)

1981—An epidemic of Dengue Hemmorhagic Fever, a painful mosquito-borne disease involving intense pain, flu symptoms, internal bleeding, and shock, strikes 300,000 Cubans and claimed 158 lives, including 101 children. A *Covert Action Information Bulletin* investigation produced evidence that the CIA released Dengue infected mosquitoes on the island (*see "Omega 7 and Dengue Fever", CAIB #22, 1984*).

1982—Dr. Wolf Szmuness, overseer of the Hep-B vaccine trials (NYC Blood Center), died of cancer and thus was unavailable to rebuke charges of foul play in connection with the numerous deaths of participants involved.

1982—Following U.S.-directed aerial bombings, Hemorrhagic Conjunctivitis mysteriously arrived in parts of El Salvador.

1983—*The New York Native*, a Gay/Lesbian weekly newspaper, published an anonymous letter to the editor from someone claiming to be a former employee of the U.S. Army Bio-warfare Laboratory at Fort Detrick, MD. The letter cites that the laboratory launched "Operation Firm Hand" in 1978 to infect homosexual men with the HIV virus.

1984—The allegedly civilian NCI "discovered" the AIDS Virus; claim of discovery, however, disputed by France. Behind closed doors, Reagan Administration officials and French government work out a compromise.

July 4, 1984—The first detailed charges of AIDS as CBW are published in *The Patriot*, New Delhi, India.

October, 1984—Soviet press picks up the story of AIDS as CBW by the U.S. military, making it easy for U.S. Defense Department spokespeople to dismiss the charges as "Soviet propaganda," but even after, the story was carried in 60 other countries and 30 different languages.

1984—*New York Native* conducted "unscientific" poll of 150 homosexual men asking whether "AIDS is actually a disease created by an arm of the federal government for political reasons." 37% agree, 45% disagree, 16% don't know (*Barry Adkins, "Time For Another Stonewall?", Nov 4-10, 1985*)

1986—Robert Strecker MD publishes *Bio-Attack Alert*, a 27 page report detailing his extensive research into the manmade origins of AIDS.

Mid-1986—Two East-German scientists, Dr. Jakob and Lilli Segal, publish a 52 page report, *AIDS-Its Nature and Origin*, arguing that HIV was genetically engineered in a U.S. CBW lab.

Oct 10th—Two "U.S. Embassy officials" visit the Segals's home. Although the officials claim credentials as a historian and political counsel, Dr. Segal stated, "I am positive they were from the CIA and that they were deeply concerned that the cover-up over the origin of AIDS was going to be exposed." The officials questioned Segal about "What he knows, what he thinks, where he got his information from, and what he intends on doing with the report." Later the State Department acknowledged sending officials, "merely to point out the fallacies of the report."

Oct 26th—*AIDS "Made in Lab" Shock*, cover story, London *Sunday Express*.

1987, March 14—M. Brussell, J. Judge, and D. Emory broadcast AIDS/BW theories; *The Secret's Out*, KPFA, Berkeley

May 11th, 1987—*Smallpox Vaccine "Triggered" AIDS Virus*, front page *London Times* account, May 11, 1987, discussed WHO smallpox vaccine/AIDS in Africa connection.

1987—AIDS pressure group, ACT-UP, forms, spearheaded by activist Larry Kramer, NYC.

1988—Alan Cantwell Jr. MD published *AIDS and the Doctors of Death* and receives excellent reviews.

1988—Suspicious and untimely deaths of three top proponents of the AIDS as CBW theory—Ted Strecker, Illinois State Rep. Douglas Huff, and activist/radio broadcaster Mae Brussell.

1988—Robert Strecker MD, produced the *The Strecker Memorandum*, a video about the man-made origins of AIDS.

1989—Debut of German film *Monkey Business, The Myth of an African Origin of AIDS, Dr. Cantwell's AIDS, and the Doctors of Death* banned at the Fifth International AIDS Conference by WHO officials.

1989—1,500 mostly black and Latino Los Angeles children were tested with Edmonstron-Zagreb, an unlicensed measles vaccine. It was also tested in a dozen third world countries. Trials were stopped when questions were raised about an increased death rate in female infants.

1990—Sept 16th; AIDS War Conference, New College, S.F

Oct 30th—*"29% of Blacks in Poll See AIDS as a Racist Plot..."* headline, *San Francisco Chronicle*. *Mixed Blood*, a play by Aubrey Hampton about the creation of AIDS, debuts at Loft Theatre, Tampa.

1993—Queer magazine *The Advocate* mocks "AIDS as CBW" theory in its *Dossier* column and refuses to print letters of dissent.

December 1st—Emergency Times Network sponsored forum on World AIDS Day, St. Petersburg, FL. Featured speaker, Dr. Dana Dennard, professor at Florida A&M University speaks on *AIDS as Covert Genocide*.

1995—Rep. Eric Taylor spearheaded petition drive for a federal court hearing on evidence of AIDS as CBW.

Chemical Biological Weapons in the U.S.

From 1960 to 1972, the U.S. Department of Defense (DOD) contracted with the University of Cincinnati to secretly experiment on U.S. citizens. The DOD wanted to study effects of massive doses of radiation on combat troops in case of nuclear war.

The government and doctors selected poor, black cancer patients and told them that they were receiving radiation treatment for their cancer. The patients were not informed about the dangerous nature of the experiments. It was also not mentioned that the radiation would hasten their deaths and cause serious suffering. Patients who had been fairly healthy had their heath decline soon after radiation treatment. Every patient died.

President Clinton revealed the deception in 1994, and press reports identified some of the victims. Family members

prosecuted the DOD. The judge hearing the case compared the Cincinnati doctors to Nazis.

Clinton offered an official apology, revealing even more instances of abuse and admitting that "thousands of government-sponsored experiments did take place at hospitals, universities, and military bases" from 1944 to 1994.

Throughout the 20th century, the U.S. government launched an aggressive campaign to monitor and assault its most vulnerable citizens. U.S. presidents, judges, legislators, and doctors proposed the forced institutionalization and sterilization of all socially unacceptable, poor women of childbearing age—to keep them from breeding.

In the early twentieth century, California vice-consulate Geza von Hoffmann urged sterilization legislation, which he saw as the "easiest measure to prevent the reproduction of inferior people." In 1894, the superintendent of a Kansas institution had already castrated 44 boys and fourteen girls, as punishment for masturbation.

Several years later, Indiana passed the first sterilization law. California followed in 1909, and eventually sterilized over sixteen thousand citizens. More than 30 states passed sterilization bills. Doctors performed covert sterilization recorded as "appendectomies" or unspecified "medical necessities."

Soon the movement became more organized, and started actively searching for targets. The Eugenics Record Office set out to locate every "defective" American citizen and assemble a government database cataloguing every "unfit" family in the country. In 1914 Harry Laughlin created a model sterilization law, and proposed sterilizing 15 million people over the next two generations. Laughlin and Charles Davenport sent out hundreds of fieldworkers from the Record Office, to gather family histories and locate potential victims.

During his presidency, Theodore Roosevelt created a "Heredity Commission" of eugenic scientists that "encourag[ed] the increase of families of good blood, and...discourag[ed]... the cross-bred American civilization." In a letter to Davenport, the president wrote, "some day we will realize that the prime duty...of the good citizen of the right type is to leave his or her blood behind him in the world; and that we have no business to permit the perpetuation of citizens of the wrong type."

The eugenicists planned to use immigration restriction, sterilization, segregation, and legislation to keep the "unfit" from breeding. Their efforts were directed against Jews, blacks, Latinos, and Indians, whom they described as "genetically inferior" to "Nordics." Laughlin was appointed the "Expert Eugenics Agent" for Congress's House Committee on Immigration and Naturalization. Representative Robert Allen summarized the movement as, "the primary reason for the restriction of the alien stream...is the necessity for purifying and keeping pure the blood of America." Laughlin called the presence of blacks in America "the worst thing that ever happened to the...United States." And Theodore Roosevelt agreed blacks were "a perfectly stupid race."

Physicians and medical students nationwide have confirmed the practice of sterilizing women through trickery or deceit. A New York hospital director admitted, "In most major teaching hospitals in NYC, it is the unwritten policy to do elective hysterectomies on poor black and Puerto Rican women...to train residents."

The Third International Congress on Eugenics was held at NYC's American Museum of Natural History on August 21-23, 1932. The press and politically active groups didn't pay much attention to it.

One of the most famous cases of secret experiments on citizens was the Tuskegee Syphillis Experiment. In 1932, U.S. Public Health Services monitored 400 men with untreated syphilis. The men were not aware of their infection, how it spreads, or its long-term effects. After the discovery of penicillin, the drug was kept from them in order for the study to continue. Eventually a federal health worker blew a whistle and the experiment was halted.

In 1969 George HW Bush was a House representative in Texas on his way to becoming the director of the CIA. He held press hearings on the "threat" posed by black babies in an apparent attempt to steer U.S. public opinion about the so-called "population bomb" in non-white areas of the world—particularly Africa. He stated that unless the menace of human population growth was "recognized and made manageable, starvation, pestilence, and war will solve it for us." Bush often compared population growth to a disease and brought two "race scientist" professors in front of a Republican task force to "objectively" discuss the subject.

In 1969, a domestic bill prohibiting biological weapons was agreed upon and passed. It contained a clause permitting defensive research and in 1972, the U.S. signed a similar international treaty, which was ratified in 1975. The Pentagon insists that these new policies meant the end of all but "defensive" biological warfare research. But the "defensive" clause strips out the intended results of the bill, as numerous CBW experts—including some of the Army's own—have attested.

In 1973, the new field of genetic engineering, combining molecules of different micro-organisms to create new viruses and bacteria, was developed through advances in scientific research. The U.S. military applied this technology to its CBW research while scientists warned of the extremely dangerous implications of such a development. Shortly afterwards, in 1976, *The Global 2000 Report* called for elimination of 1/3 of the world's population by the year 2000.

How was the U.S. Government and CIA Involved?

The Soviet news agency *TASS* has repeatedly charged that the U.S. military created AIDS in laboratory experiments for the development of biological warfare. The story, reported by Dan

Rather on the March 30, 1987 edition of *CBS Evening News*, was denied by the U.S. government, as it has been repeatedly since such allegations first appeared in 1986. Since that time, the Soviets have charged that biological warfare research was carried out at Ft. Detrick, Maryland, in violation of the tenets of the Geneva Convention.

The Patriot Newspaper claimed that Fort Detrick scientists, with the help of the Centers for Disease Control, and under Pentagon contract, traveled to Zaire, Nigeria, and Latin America, to collect information on "a powerful virus that could not be found in Europe or Asia." According to a summary of the Patriot article in a Soviet journal, this information was then "analyzed at Ft. Detrick, and the result was the isolation of a new virus that causes AIDS...certain experiments were probably done in Haiti and in certain groups of the American population, beginning with homosexuals, drug users, homeless, etc."

Between 1972 and 1977 Jakob and Lilli Segal, two East German scientists, spliced the Visna virus (believed to be the mother of the AIDS virus), a sheep retrovirus, with HTLV-1, the first retrovirus known to affect humans. It was created at the CBW labs in Fort Detrick, Maryland. The base at Ft. Detrick was called the "Army Biological Warfare Laboratory" until Nixon's 1969 order banning CBW production. Fort Detrick was then the leading center for development of testing of biological weapons.

Shortly after the CBW "ban," part of the grounds were, with great fanfare, renamed the "Frederick Cancer Research Facility" and turned over to the National Cancer Institute for civilian use. The military section was later renamed the "U.S. Army Medical Research Institute for Infectious Disease" (USAMUD), supposedly restricted to "defensive" research. But underneath the slick name changes, CBW research continued.

According to one scientist's account, "Within two years of its foundation, the Institute's staff and budget had tripled." In 1969, a military official testified before Congress: "Within the next 5 or 10 years, it would probably be possible to make a new infective micro-organism which could differ in certain important respects from any known disease causing organisms. Most important of these is that it might be refractory (resistant to the immunological and therapeutic processes upon which we depend to maintain our relative freedom from infectious disease.)"

The U.S. Department of Defense Appropriations 1969-1970 library call #Y4.AP6/1:D36/5/970/ PART 6 HB 15090 called for, and allocated funds for, the creation of a killer virus with the clinical description of AIDS. This coincides with a 1975 prediction by Jay Corbenson that turned out to be deathly accurate. He was a guest speaker at an international assembly of cancer researchers in Japan and said, "You are going to have an epidemic—a worldwide epidemic—a pandemic, of a virus that would cause cancer." He didn't refer to it as AIDS, he called it "a virus that causes cancer" which is exactly what AIDS is. How was he able to make such an accurate prediction just as military funding was paying for the development of such a virus?

In February, 1987, a lawsuit by the foundation for Economic Trends, a Washington, D.C. environmental group, forced the Department of Defense (DOD) to admit the operation of CBW research programs—"defensive" of course—at 127 sites around the country, including universities, foundations, and corporations. The DOD had not examined the health effort of these activities, as required by law. The committee made public CIA documents showing that the agency had a vast array of poisons, including many that would cause deadly diseases, and systems for destroying crops.

It was in the secret project that two poisons, one a toxin made from shellfish, the other a derivative of cobra venom, were stockpiled by the CIA in violation of President Nixon's directive, William Colby, former director of Central Intelligence, said. They also made public the "Draft Environmental Impact Statement/Biological Defense Research Program" which listed the most dangerous biological weapons experiments being conducted at Dugway Proving Ground, Aberdeen Proving Ground, and Fort Detrick.

Colby said that in May, 1952, the CIA began a joint project with the special operations division of the Army Biological Laboratory at Fort Detrick. During the course of this project, his testimony and documents disclosed that the CIA stockpiled substances that would cause tuberculosis, anthrax, encephalitis, valley fever, salmonella, food poisoning, and small pox.

Colby said that the project had been subject to a high degree of secrecy within the CIA. Only two or three officers at any given time were cleared for access to Ft. Detrick activities. Jeremy Rifkin was a scientist at Ft. Detrick who left his job on grounds of conscience. He tells the story of a team leader losing an entire quart of Chicungunya virus, sufficient to kill a major portion of humanity. The military has never been able to account for where the virus ended up. They say, "Well, it can't be missing because we can't find it."

The Army admits it has "infectious disease research institutes" in Kenya and Brazil. Brazil has the second highest number of AIDS cases—after the U.S.—in the Western Hemisphere. In an attempt to refute the charges coming from the press in every country but the U.S., David L. Huxsoll, the chief at U.S Army Medial Research Institute for Infectious Disease (part of Fort Detrick) said that once AIDS surfaced, they screened it as they do any infectious agent. He said they had "definitely looked at it," and "...studies at the Army laboratories have shown that the AIDS virus would be an extremely poor biological warfare agent."

These statements seem to incriminate AIDS testing at Fort Detrick rather than distancing from wrong doing. Huxsoll later denied these statements.

Then there is the case of Philip Agee, a former CIA agent. After defecting, his 1975 book *Inside the Company* explained the depths that the agency goes to: "Even after recent revelations about the CIA it is still difficult for people to understand what a huge and sinister organization the CIA is. It is the biggest and most powerful secret service that has ever existed. I don't know how big the KGB is inside the Soviet Union, but its international operation is small compared with the CIA's. The CIA has 16,500 employees and an annual budget of $750,000,000. That does not include its mercenary armies or its commercial subsidiaries. Add them all together, the agency employs or subsidizes hundreds of thousands of people and spends billions every year. Its official budget is secret; it's concealed in those of other Federal agencies. Nobody tells Congress what the CIA spends. By law, the CIA is not accountable to Congress."

"In the past 25 years, the CIA has been involved in plots to overthrow governments in Iran, the Sudan, Syria, Guatemala, Ecuador, Guyana, Zaire, and Ghana. It also made a lot of effort destabilizing governments and putting oppressive regimes and coups in power. In Cuba, The Company paid for and directed the invasion that failed at the Bay of Pigs. Some time later the CIA was involved in numerous attempts to assassinate Fidel Castro."

In 1996, through declassified documents, court testimony, and interviews conducted by Gary Webb, it was discovered that a CIA operation was instrumental in putting cheap cocaine into black communities in the early 1980s. Two fundraisers for the contras, Norwin Menesel and Danilo Blandon, while enjoying protection from investigation and prosecution, brought the first cheap and large scale cocaine into South-Central Los Angeles.

Hep-B Vaccinations in Manhattan, San Francisco, and Los Angeles

The initial U.S. epicenter for AIDS was New York City, shortly after a 1978 Hep-B vaccine study was conducted on gay men. The government recruited male participants for their study through ads in queer publications. The requirements were that participants be between 20 and 40 years old, homosexual or bisexual, healthy, and *promiscuous*. After screening the blood of about 10,000 men, a final group of 1,083 were selected to participate in the study. The gay men selected were mostly white and college educated, had an average age of 29, and mostly had no history of venereal disease.

In January 1979, two months after the New York City Hepatitis vaccine trials, the first case of AIDS was discovered in a young gay man there. In March 1980, the western vaccine trials on gay men—with the same specifications as in Manhattan— began in Los Angeles and San Francisco. Seven months later, the first cases of AIDS were detected in those cities. The CDC published a report in August 1981 containing the following data on the first 26 AIDS cases: All were homosexual/ bisexual men, 20 were from New York City, six were from Los Angles or San Francisco, the average age was 29, and most were well educated. Perhaps the similarities in these two data pools is what caused the U.S. Department of Justice to keep this information classified from the public. But why would this new virus only affect young white male homosexuals selectively in Manhattan, San Francisco, and Los Angeles?

One volunteer in the experiment who was injected with the Hep-B vaccine recalled being taken into a room to be injected. The nurse said "Oh, don't worry. We're not giving you anything that will make you sick." He remembers being told that a couple of times and after the injection he regretted being a part of the study. He was convinced it was an experimentation of viruses that got out of hand. While he was talking publicly about his experience, most of the people that were in the Hep-B study had already died of AIDS. No outcomes of the Hep-B study were ever published. After much protesting, he was promised a newsletter updating him on plans and results of the study but it never arrived. His friends in the study continued to die around him without any published results.

According to the study, the supposed effectiveness rating for the tests was 96%. Recent studies have shown that Hep-B vaccination is not very successful in immuno-depressed people. In HIV-positive individuals, the success rate of the Hep-B vaccine is about 50%, only protecting one out of two people infected with the AIDS virus. The gay men in the study were healthy before the experiment—and damaged afterward. The experiment would have been a failure if the immune systems of the men had been infected with HIV and not working at full capacity. This would indicate how the men tested healthy but were getting sick and dying shortly afterwards.

By 1981, 40% of the Hep-B vaccination patients had AIDS and by 1984, 64% did. After that figure health officials would no longer release the statistics. A prominent California doctor who pointed out the mortality rate for the Hep-B program participants, as reported by the WHO, matched World War 2 and then he was promptly and mysteriously murdered.

Corrupt Research, Funding, Media Focus, Mysterious Deaths

The total tax dollars spent on AIDS exceeded $50 billion by the year 2000. Annual funding increases every year and is one of the few areas of the budget that didn't see any threat of cuts for many years. A high priority was given to AIDS based on the activists of ACT UP in the 1980s and the widespread fear and assumption that AIDS is a growing health threat to all Americans. Government institutions are responsible for generating official AIDS reports and are often the recipients of these billions of dollars in AIDS spending. Predictably, their findings and reports support increased funding for AIDS research. A CDC virologist, Dr. Walter Dowdle, admitted, "As long as this was seen as a gay disease, or even worse, a disease of drug abusers, this pushed the disease way down the ladder [of funding priorities]." Despite spending over $50 billion in federal funding we still lack significant areas of understanding

how HIV and AIDS behave and their abnormalities.

The CDC made an early decision to inflate AIDS estimates and magnify the risks involved. This launched an advertising campaign causing a full scale epidemic to seem likely in two years. By 1991, misinformation had caused the public to believe that married couples were at risk of contracting AIDS even though AIDS rarely infected anyone beyond IV drug users and queer men. Federal tax dollars allocated to AIDS doubled the first year of the ad campaign and by the early '90s they were topping over a billion dollars a year in advertising.

There are about 90,000 AIDS organizations in the U.S.; that works out to be about one organization for every six people diagnosed with AIDS.

Ted Strecker, Robert Strecker's brother, on the verge of disseminating powerful information about the man-made nature of the AIDS virus, was found shot to death alone in his home in Springfield, Missouri, an apparent suicide, on August 11, 1988. In the past, Ted suffered from depression and monumental frustration at the relative lack of interest in his findings. Dr. Strecker spoke with him the night before his death. Ted was cheerful, in good spirits, and looking forward to certain new developments that promised progress. The next day he was found dead, his 22-caliber rifle next to him. No note, no message, no good-byes to anyone; very atypical of him. But officially a suicide.

Illinois State Representative Douglas Huff of Chicago was also found dead and alone in his home, seemingly after an overdose of cocaine and heroin, on September 22, 1988.

Representative Huff had worked hard to make the Illinois State Legislature and the people of Chicago aware of Dr. Strecker's work. His cause of death was officially listed as a stroke. Friends and associates are skeptical of either case as a candidate for suicide.

In a related development, Minnesota's gay newsweekly *GLC Voice* received an anonymous letter from "a friend of the family," a self-admitted researcher at the Pentagon's Biological Weapons Research Department. *GLC Voice*, which was quick to point out that the letter offers no facts to assist an investigative reporter to verify its allegations, printed the letter nonetheless. In it the author states he was involved with "technically illegal and supposedly nonexistent" research ten years ago, developing "biological agents that kill quickly and efficiently, and others designed to produce a very low, debilitating death. The virus that causes AIDS is of the latter variety."

Smallpox vaccines and AIDS in Africa and Brazil

On May 11, 1987, a headline appeared on the cover of the *London Times* proclaiming "Smallpox Vaccine Triggered AIDS Virus." It was written by science editor Pierce Wright and suggested that the smallpox eradication program sponsored by the World Health Organization (WHO) was responsible for unleashing AIDS in Africa. On June 5, Jon Rappoport, an investigative reporter, examined the article in a short piece he wrote for the *LA Weekly*. Rappoport was mystified as to the lack of mentions of the smallpox story in U.S. media and contacted spokespersons for the largest newswires in the U.S. All of the agencies said that they had heard nothing of the story out of London.

AIDS researcher Robert Strecker MD, was aware of the story that ran in Europe and spoke to representatives at AP and UPI newswires, asking why the story wasn't carried in the U.S. According to Strecker "they were not able to understand the significance of the article." Between 1966 and 1977 the WHO carried out large scale vaccinations for Smallpox across Africa and Brazil shortly before the first appearance of AIDS there. This became potentially concerning when the WHO's information indicates that the AIDS table of Central Africa matches the concentration and distribution of smallpox vaccinations. The greatest spread of HIV infection coincides with the most intense immunization programs. Thus, Zaire, at the top of the AIDS list, had 36 million people immunized with the smallpox vaccine. Next is Zambia, with 19 million, followed by Tanzania with 15 million, Uganda with 11 million, Malawai with 8 million, Ruanda with 3.3 million, and Burundi with 3.2 million. Brazil, the only South American country covered by the smallpox eradication campaign, had the highest incidence of AIDS in that part of the world.

An unnamed WHO advisor disclosed to the *Times*: "I thought it was just a coincidence until we studied the latest findings about the reactions which can be caused by vaccinia. Now I believe the smallpox vaccine theory is the explanation to the explosion of AIDS." This theory could explain how AIDS infection is spread more evenly between males and females in Africa than in the West. Further links between AIDS and the smallpox vaccine come from the Walter Reed Army Medical Center in Washington, D.C., where routine smallpox vaccination of a 19-year-old army recruit was the trigger for the stimulation of dormant HIV virus into full-blown AIDS.

Government scientists have been quick to point the finger at peoples' lifestyles: "You don't have the right sexual partners," "You don't wear enough condoms," etc. Government doctors are also quick to blame IV drug users for spreading AIDS by sharing needles. But in the WHO's smallpox vaccination campaign, the same needles were re-used 40 to 60 times and the main method of "sterilization" was waving the needle across a flame.

No follow-up data is available from the smallpox eradication campaign because no systematic studies of the complications of the mass immunization were done. Dr. Laurence Godis said, "Previous circumstantial evidence looks more persuasive alongside the latest research that shows AIDS can be stimulated by smallpox vaccination."

The definition of AIDS in Africa differs decisively from the one used in the U.S. and Europe. Due to lack of healthcare facilities, it is more reliable to identify AIDS by defining characteristics such as diarrhea, fever, persistent cough, and weight loss greater than 10% over two months. The problem is that due to malnutrition, poor drinking water, and a lack of access to basic antibiotics, this set of symptoms has appeared together much longer than the AIDS virus has "existed." It is hard to distinguish what is "slim" (slang for AIDS) and what is a result of unrelated poor health. Dr. Chifumbe Chintu explains the problem this creates as, "Africans with treatable medical conditions, such as tuberculosis, who perceive themselves as having HIV infection, fail to seek medical attention because they think they have an untreatable disease." In Uganda most people can't afford medication or healthcare. Many in Africa simply do not have access to healthcare.

In villages where visits to a hospital are nonexistent all death is considered "slim" or AIDS, driving up statistics. If someone dies from malaria or herpes it is attributed to AIDS. Even accidental deaths are sometimes attributed to AIDS. Parasitic infections, tuberculosis, cholera, and many other diseases are indistinguishable from what is summarized as AIDS.

On a trip to Africa, Celia Farber, a reporter for *Spin Magazine* observed that everywhere that "AIDS" existed in Africa there was also money; a brand new clinic with a new Mercedes parked outside, modern testing facilities, high paying jobs, and international conferences. A leading African practicing physician warned that the reporters would never get the truth from the doctors as half of their annual pay is per diems for attending AIDS conferences and playing the game: Doing what they are told. The success of AIDS activism in the west seemingly had driven funding corruption from one extreme to the other.

Unlike in Manhattan in the 1980s, funding for AIDS research in Africa is highly disproportionate to other diseases that are more deadly. The WHO allotted $6 million dollars in Uganda for a year of AIDS research while all other diseases, except TB, received a combined $57,000, even while Malaria was the leading killer of people worldwide.

On her way home from Africa, Farber spoke to a man who had worked with a water restoration program in Kenya for six months. He explained how people were sick from dirty drinking water when he arrived, "They had the most atrocious diarrhea and vomiting and abdominal pains." When she asked him how long this had been going on he replied "about ten years" and when she asked if the symptoms went away after the water was cleaned his answer was, "Oh, absolutely."

Scientists in the U.S. successfully linked the cause of AIDS in Africa to theories of children playing with dead monkeys, but the disease in Africa began in cities, not in the jungle. Also curiously, the genetic makeup of the AIDS virus does not exist in modern primates. Viruses have not been known to change forms

and "jump" to a different species since ancient times. Aside from the fact that it's virtually impossible that the disease came from monkeys, the initial HIV outbreak in Africa affected only black Africans, not white ones.

Africans thought to have AIDS are horribly stigmatized, sometimes banished from their villages and left to die, often with no treatment for their symptoms, even if they do make it to a hospital. An AIDS diagnosis is an unspeakable horror; a death sentence. Because the publicity campaigns have portrayed AIDS as a sexually transmitted disease, a diagnosis comes with the guilt of irresponsibility.

Despite Funding, Answers Aren't Quite Clear

New data shows distinct differences in the molecular structure of the human and monkey viruses, first reported by the University of Tokyo. "Although inter-species transmission may have occurred in ancient times" the report, written by Masashi Fukasawa, stated, "there appears to have been no transmission 'for a long time.'"

Dr. Robert Strecker of California says, "It must have been genetically engineered." Dr. John Seale, described by the *Sunday Express* as a "distinguished London based specialist," said, "I am now totally convinced that the AIDS virus [sic] is man-made."

In West Germany, Professor Jakob Segal pinpointed Ft. Detrick as the most likely place to conduct the engineering necessary to create a synthesized virus. Segal, retired director of the Institute of Biology at Berlin University, is said to be compiling a 55-page report expounding his conviction that HIV is man-made and that there has been "a cover up of the blunders which unleashed a medical catastrophe on the world." According to the *Sunday Express*, two U.S. Embassy officials questioned Segal at his home for two hours about his information. Segal maintains that, although the two had credentials as a historian and a political counsel, he is "positive they were from the CIA—and that they were deeply concerned that the cover up of the origin of AIDS was going to be exposed." Seale told the *Sunday Express* that, although Segal is from East Berlin, "he holds no particular political beliefs or views at all."

Regarding the theory that the origin of AIDS stems from infected African green monkeys, Segal said, "It's ludicrous and scientifically incredible—and has been promoted, I believe, by the United States government as part of the cover up."

Dr. John Seale, a Fellow of the Royal Society of Medicine and former consultant in venerology at the Middlesex and St. Thoms's Hospitals in London, said he did not necessarily agree with Segal that the virus was created in a military establishment, believing instead that "it is more likely to have been an ordinary laboratory where cancer research is being carried out." He is no less emphatic than Segal in his "firm conviction...that a scientist... probably in the United States and doing cancer research with the two viruses, accidentally spliced elements of both together—and created AIDS."

Strecker, who has been studying AIDS since the first cases were reported, says, "There is no known animal virus with all the symptoms of AIDS; it must have been genetically engineered, from different viruses. The two viruses which were used, according to all my research and studies, are Maedi-Visna and Bovine Leukemia.

Segal believes "that scientists here [at Ft. Detrick]

created the AIDS virus by combining parts of the Maedi-Visna virus and "another leukemia virus, HTLV-1," first named by Dr. Robert Gallo of the National Cancer Institute (NCI). "Almost certainly the scientists were unaware of their terrible creation—the AIDS virus."

"In the mid-1970s, experiments were carried out at Ft. Detrick when the U.S. Army Medical Research Command had its headquarters on volunteer long-term prisoners who were promised freedom after the test. We all know that it takes years from the time of infection to the time of serious illness and death from AIDS. After the prisoners were injected with the newly made virus, there would have been no immediate signs of illness, and they would have been released as promised into the world." Segal's account coincides with the first known case of AIDS in 1978.

The 1988 Defense Department "Draft Environmental Impact Statement/Biological Defense Research Program" was made available to *Examiner* reporter Vicki Haddock as a result of a lawsuit filed by Jeremy Rifkin, an opponent of the Pentagon's bio-warfare studies. The statement says the most dangerous biological weapons experiments are being conducted at three U.S. Army bases: Dugway Proving Ground, Utah; Aberdeen Proving Ground, Maryland; and Fort Detrick, Maryland. Dr. Robert Strecker explained how this would be done in a laboratory in a speech: "So, what kind of name would you give it if it's a hybrid of bovine and visna? Well, we called it bovine-visna and we called it visna-bovine. We went to the library and we set out on a Medline search: 'Give me every paper ever written from 1900 on bovine-visna virus and visna-bovine virus.' This is exactly what you can do if you want to spend the $35-and bam! Off they came: Papers from the early 1970s on a virus named bovine-visna—it has the exact same shape as the AIDS virus, it has the exact same morphology, it has the exact same magnesium dependency, the ability to produce in tissue culture, the selective ability to kill T-cells in tissue culture. And when they fed that virus from cows naturally infected with it to chimpanzees, those chimpanzees died of pneumocystis carinii pneumonia. That's AIDS."

"The Maedi-Visna virus is a slow infectious virus causing wasting of the body, progressive destruction of the brain and lungs, and loss of weight. The Bovine Leukemia virus would cause immune deficiency and the formation of solid white cells in the brain."

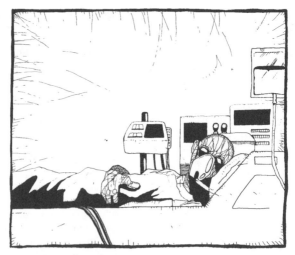

"Visna is a sheep virus which is believed to be the mother of the AIDS virus—you find visna was causing 3 types of lesions in mice in the late 1970s. We wrote many years ago, in 1985, 1986, that AIDS was clearly related to cancer and it was a cancer-causing agent." "If you go to the medical library and put in AIDS, where does all the literature start? It starts around '82, '83. Because before '81 the virus wasn't even 'discovered.' You've got to go to the veterinarian literature. The veterinarians have been laughing at the doctors for years now...If you want to know about AIDS, talk to your vet—they work with cattle and sheep."

The Decline of AIDS

In 1986 *Newsweek* warned "by 1991, HIV, in all probability, will have spread to between five and 10 million Americans." But it never happened. The estimates steadily went down to continual new lows since AIDS was discovered.

By 2003, 410,800 people died of AIDS while heart disease claimed 14 million. This figure also includes accidents, non-contagious illnesses, drug side effect deaths, and other indirect causes of death in people diagnosed with AIDS. AIDS is no longer among the top ten causes of death for Americans. Even when AIDS was reported as the leading cause of death among Americans ages 25-44, only .2% of this age group die from any cause each year and AIDS represents 15% of these deaths. It was a demographic that is not likely to die from other means.

And in the last 20 years, CDC statistics show that AIDS has not spread outside the original risk groups of individuals. As a result of the hard work of activist groups like ACT UP, proper research funding has been applied and cases have decreased until it was no longer an epidemic in the queer community.

Chemical Biological Weapons & the Origins, History, and the future of AIDS

Why are new retroviral diseases, never before seen in modern medicine, appearing so soon after retroviruses were "discovered?" Why did the AIDS "supervirus" appear a decade after it was predicted by the bio-warfare experts? Why is Kaposi's sarcoma the leading form of cancer in gay men with AIDS? What is the role of mycoplasma and cancer microbes in AIDS and why is this research not being funded?

It is frightening to see the result of the Hep-B vaccine study not released, to see media/wire stories killed, and for key figures to be overtaken by mysterious and conveniently timed deaths; but it is outright horrifying to put all of the evidence into context and look at the scope of the problem.

It seems that only with a more complex understanding of the disease—its nature and origins—will the problem ever be fully understood or adequately addressed. Despite all of this evidence, prevention methods, including condoms and clean needles, are still very necessary for living a healthy lifestyle—and to prevent other diseases.

Sources/Other Reading:

The Oregonian July 26, 1998

AIDS: Words From the Front, *Spin*, March 1993, Celia Farber

Science Fiction, *Gear*, March 2000, Celia Farber

Inventing the AIDS Virus, PH Duesberg, Regnery Publishing 1996

AIDS Acquired by Drug Consumption and Other Non-Contagious Risk Factors, PH Duesberg, North Atlantic Books 1996

Queer Blood, Alan Cantwell

Chemical Biological Warfare, Medical Experiments, and Population Control, Robert Lederer Dr. Robert Strecker, speech delivered to University of CA at Santa Barbara, May 25, 1990

AIDS Linked to Smallpox Vaccine, Robert S Meddelson, MD, Dec, 1987

Research Refutes Idea that Human AIDS Virus Originated in Monkeys, Robert Steinbrook, *Los Angeles Times*, June 2, 1988

Soviet Allegations Resurface that U.S. Military Created AIDS, New York Native, Mike Salinas, April 18, 1987

Inside the Company: CIA Diary Phillip Agee, 1975

The CIA Makes Scien

A look at the way the PATRIOT act and p
9/11 "security" changed our civil libert
and infringed upon basic American righ

Fiction Unexciting #3

"They that can give up essential liberty to obtain a little temporary safety deserve neither liberty nor safety."
—*Benjamin Franklin*

FISA: The Foreign Intelligence Surveillance Act

In 1978 Congress passed the Foreign Intelligence Surveillance Act to prevent U.S. government intelligence abuses against U.S. citizens. But for over thirty years, paranoid law enforcement and intelligence officials spied on Americans and searched their possessions without permission. Approaching the turn of the millennium, U.S. Presidents declared an "implicit authority" to spy without a warrant, for the sake of "national security."

But by the 1970s, the Weather Underground and Church Committee had exposed and documented extreme government abuses during the 1960s: The FBI's harassment and illegal wiretapping of law-abiding protesters and civil rights leaders; CIA and NSA operations; and Watergate. The CIA had compiled files on over 13,000 individuals, detailing 1,000 domestic organizations and over 7,000 U.S. citizens. The Committee found this spying to be excessive, undemocratic, and violating the Constitution.

The resulting public outrage, on top of fears that this information would force the outlawing of warrantless surveillance, led Gerald Ford to compromise with the FISA bill. Instead of outlawing political policing by the Department of Justice (DOJ) and intelligence agencies, the government required spying to go through a legal process. The bill was drafted behind closed doors, approved by Congress, and approved by President Jimmy Carter—giving birth to a secret federal court in 1978.

FISA was a deal between civil libertarians and the federal government. It was easier to monitor foreign spies, but supposedly required court oversight, with the intended function being to avoid persecution of American citizens for legal activities.

The clandestine Foreign Intelligence Surveillance Court (FISC) was created to issue warrant-less surveillance orders. The FISC secretly approves electronic surveillance applications to wiretap phones and conduct physical searches, "for the purpose of obtaining foreign intelligence information." The process is—of course—secret. FISA subjects typically never know they have been monitored or had their property searched.

FISA surveillance orders are called "warrants," but a search warrant is issued because of probable cause that a crime is likely. Unlike criminal warrants, FISA orders do not need probable cause that a subject is involved with a crime, or that a search is expected to result in criminal evidence.

FISA was meant to create a "wall" between criminal investigations and intelligence gathering. After infractions against U.S. citizens, Congress specified that the FISA should authorize *only* surveillance of "agents of a foreign power." In order to spy on American citizens, the DOJ must show probable cause that the suspect is engaged in criminal espionage. FISA was meant for use against spies, international terrorists, and enemies of the U.S.—to separate intelligence investigations from prosecutions of other kinds of crime.

Isn't There Always A Catch?

FISA surveillance and search orders, as well as evidence obtained by them, are top-secret. An agent can sneak into a suspect's house, search it, and leave in complete secrecy. If the search reveals evidence that leads to a prosecution, the warrant and the reason it was granted are kept secret—and therefore impossible to challenge—if the Attorney General claims that the information pertains to "national security."

If a defendant tries to challenge or suppress evidence obtained through FISA surveillance, the defendant, the attorney, and the public are all typically permanently refused access to any FISA materials. Even though decisions of the court can result in criminal charges, a FISA target cannot dispute evidence or allegations against them.

Congressional oversight of FISC is virtually nonexistent. The Attorney General's office must give Congress annual and semi-annual reports with the number of FISA applications requested, granted, and denied. These reports are about two paragraphs.

In its 34-year history, the court has processed over 20,000 applications for surveillance, and denied exactly *four* applications. The denials came in 2003, after rampant FISA abuse was revealed in 2002.

FISA surveillance orders have exploded exponentially. Since 2003, the FISC issued more surveillance and search orders than all other federal courts combined. Defense attorneys call the FISC a "court of last resort" for prosecutors who can't get search warrants or prosecutions from Constitutionally-protected courts.

Gaining Momentum

During Clinton's administration, FISC's authority and reported abuses grew significantly. Previously, FISA was limited to electronic eavesdropping and wiretapping, but in 1995 it was expanded to include covert, warrantless physical entries, and searches of property.

This expansion allowed evidence from FISA to be used in criminal trials. Interestingly, after the 1995 expansion, the Supreme Court ruled that the Constitution requires individuals be given notice that their belongings have been searched by the government. But because FISA searches are carried out in secret and difficult to challenge in court, the same laws did not seem to apply to FISA.

In 1998, FISA was further amended to permit pen/trap orders and monitoring of business records. The Bush and Obama administrations have continued this pattern and dramatically increased the secret court's powers. In 2001, the USA PATRIOT Act (UPA) used semantics to drastically change FISA's purpose and repercussions.

The UPA changed the "purpose of the surveillance is to obtain foreign intelligence information" to "a *significant* purpose of the surveillance." Surveillance of Americans was no longer limited to suspected spies. The FISA process can be used as a tool of arrest and prosecution by law enforcement.

The Bush administration increased the length of time of FISA surveillance from 24 to 72 hours before getting a court order. It increased FISC judges from seven to eleven.

In 2005 the FISC approved 2,072 applications to spy on non-criminal Americans, while all federal judges combined

approved 1,773 requests to investigate criminals.

Since its creation in 1978, politicians have gradually removed the protections granted to U.S. citizens by FISA.

1979: 207 FISA applications, 0 denied
1994: 576 FISA applications, 0 denied
1996: 839 FISA applications, 0 denied
1999: 886 FISA applications, 0 denied
2000: 1,012 FISA applications, 0 denied
2002: 1,228 FISA applications, 2 denied, but both reversed on appeal.
2003: 1,728 FISA applications, 4 denied.
2004: 1,758 FISA applications, 0 denied.
2005: 2,072 FISA applications, 0 denied.

Court Structure

Each judge serves a non-renewable seven-year term, arranged so that a new member is brought in every year with at least one judge from a district court in the Washington, D.C. area.

The FISC meets two days monthly. Each judge reviews applications submitted by the Attorney General. They sit in a sealed, windowless, vault-like chamber on the top floor of the DOJ headquarters. Hearings are held in this secret courtroom behind cipher-locked doors—guarded at all times—and frequently inspected for bugs.

Once the FISC judge approves an application, electronic surveillance can be initiated for 90-365 days before extensions are granted.

FISA Orders against U.S. Targets

FBI, NSA, and CIA operatives' FISA requests must state why the surveillance target is believed to be an "agent of a foreign power," how surveillance will be performed, and have a "certification" from a high-ranking executive branch official that "deems the information sought to be foreign intelligence information."

In the event that the FISC judge denies a FISA application, the decision can be reversed by the three-member FISA Court of Review (this has happened exactly once, in 2002). If the Appeals Court denies the application (hasn't happened yet), then the case can be presented to the final jurisdiction of the Supreme Court.

FISA proceedings are one-sided, with the government presenting its case against unrepresented citizens. Judgments are based on the DOJ's presentations and claims. Agents do not have to report back on their surveillance activities.

Agent Of A Foreign Power

A "foreign power" is any "foreign-based political organization" or "any group engaged in international terrorism or activities in preparation therefore." For an American to be targeted, "probable cause" must exist to show that the U.S. person spies for a foreign power, or that their activities "may" or "are about to" involve an espionage-related crime. An agent of a foreign power "knowingly aids or abets any person in the conduct of [certain] activities."

Suppose you attend a mosque under FBI surveillance. Suppose, unbeknownst to you, that your roommate, lover, or friend had associations with some foreign government or made statements threatening the government. Suppose your employer works for a foreign government. Suppose someone spreads a rumor that you made terrorist threats. You are then legally part of a "terrorist network" and can be placed under surveillance according to the FISA. Your emails, home, car, library records, medical records, and business records can be secretly monitored and searched indefinitely.

If the FBI obtains a FISA warrant to put someone under surveillance, evidence of a crime is forwarded to investigators. Law enforcement can begin its own investigations and gather evidence that will be admissible in court.

In a 2003 Judiciary Committee Report, a bipartisan group of senators noted that FBI agents who dealt with FISA didn't understand the definitions of "probable cause" or "agent of a foreign power." An investigation revealed that neither FBI agents nor attorneys "have a clear understanding of the legal standard for probable cause...This is such a basic legal principle that...it is impossible to justify the FBI's lack of complete and proper training on it."

The senators described a closed hearing in which a key FBI Headquarters Supervisory Special Agent, assigned to terrorism matters, stated that not only did he not know "probable cause" was necessary to get a FISA warrant, but he did not understand what "probable cause" meant. The supervising unit chief also admitted that he neither understood probable cause nor the "agent of a foreign power" requirement in his own testimony.

The report describes how "a very senior attorney from the FBI's Office of General Counsel with national security responsibilities" admitted that the FBI did not have written procedures defining "probable cause" in FISA cases. The attorney stated: "On the FISA side of the house, I don't think we have any written guidelines on that," before conceding, "[w]e need to have some kinds of facts that an agent can swear to a reasonable belief that they are true," to demonstrate that suspect is an agent of a foreign power.

The senators accused the DOJ and FBI of asking Congress to relax FISA standards instead of improving or reforming their own institutional training and leadership. Nonetheless, the government continued expansion of FISA's powers while lessening its requirements. Michael Chertoff and John Ashcroft testified that after the USA PATRIOT Act was passed, the DOJ pressured Congress to continue relaxing FISA requirements, including expansion of the definition of "foreign power." But, the report states, "when asked to provide this Committee with information about specific cases that support your claim to need such broad new powers, DOJ was silent in its response and named no specific cases showing such a need, nor did it say that it could provide such specificity, even in a classified setting."

Hint: FISA Is Not Constitutional.

The 1995 expansion of the FISC allows government agents to scour a target's home, papers, and effects indiscriminately and without probable cause of any crime. Foreign intelligence investigations are not required to satisfy 4th Amendment requirements, because the information wasn't intended to bring someone to justice, only to use for counterintelligence.

The Fourth Amendment warrant requirement prevents government from harassing citizens by fabricating, planting, or hypothesizing evidence, and then prosecution on that evidence without allowing it to be contested. But the way FISC plays out allows precisely these scenarios.

FISA's court secrecy allows the FBI and NSA to control what information is presented. The feds hold the proverbial cards while owning the casino. FISA orders play out as fishing expeditions. "We often don't know what we're looking for when we go in," said Deputy Attorney General Jamie Gorelick. The FISA review court has admitted that FISA orders do not meet the Fourth Amendment requirements of probable cause or describing seized items seized and creating records of places searched. The court justifies this because its searches supposedly involve "national security." But false or flimsy "counterintelligence" reports tend to be used to get warrants for law enforcement to spy in cases where probable cause of a crime does not exist.

The FISA court allows the government to conduct searches they would not be allowed to conduct under the traditional constitutional provisions. If officers fail to secure a search warrant under traditional constitutional arguments, they can go to the FISA court, and convert the case artificially into a national security investigation, securing approval for the same search.

In 1972, The Supreme Court ruled that the Fourth Amendment prohibits warrantless surveillance of domestic

targets. The Court warned against the government's use of "national security" as a pretext for surveillance, and sees surveillance as an especially grave intrusion.

Because of the "tendency of those who execute the criminal laws...to obtain conviction by means of unlawful seizures," the Supreme Court states, "Few threats to liberty exist which are greater than those posed by the use of eavesdropping devices."

The Court continues, if "neither a warrant nor a statute authorizing eavesdropping can be drawn so as to meet the Fourth Amendment's requirements...then the 'fruits' of eavesdropping devices are barred under the Amendment."

The Fourth Amendment requires that a warrant be issued by a "neutral and detached magistrate." The FISA review court insists that a FISA judge fits this definition. However, since all proceedings are top-secret and not one case was refused for the first 25 years and more than 10,000 surveillance orders, the supposed neutrality of the FISA judge position seems questionable.

Despite the First Amendment, a U.S. citizen may be spied on for political statements and views, personal relationships, business associations, status, or religion. Thousands of American citizens are monitored because of associations with FISA targets. Surveillance devices are continuous and without oversight, allowing people not named by FISA orders to be recorded for long periods of time.

When those under surveillance believe that their conversations, communications, and belongings are private—but are actually being recorded, analyzed, and searched by the government—they are being deprived of the Fifth Amendment right not to act as a witness against oneself.

The sealed nature of FISA evidence additionally violates a citizen's Sixth Amendment rights to confront accusers, to review evidence against him or her, and to legal counsel.

Not surprisingly, in each case where a defendant challenged FISA evidence, the petition was denied for "national security." Because U.S. courts are forced to become instruments of government agents, judges must take the DOJ's word regarding evidence, thus violating the independence of the judiciary.

During the Clinton Administration, the FISC used its powers to get financial information and data for political party contributors. As the late Supreme Court Justice William Brennan said, "The concept of military necessity is seductively broad, and...there is always a temptation to invoke security 'necessities' to justify an encroachment upon civil liberties."

In Action

Few FISA cases become public record but a handful have, and they illustrate how FISA has been used.

In October 1993, without issuing a warrant, Janet Reno approved a search of the home of CIA spy Aldrich Ames. After months of wiretapping Ames, breaking into his car, and searching his office and family trash, FBI agents made keys to his house in order to enter it.

Legal scholars and ACLU lawyers claimed this was unconstitutional so the DOJ rushed to validate the search, simultaneously expanding its powers by asking Congress to permanently allow the FISC to conduct physical searches. Clinton approved the FISA's 1995 expansion. The Supreme Court, however, ruled in a different case that the Constitution requires individuals to be given notice that their belongings had been searched by the government.

In another case, people who were not targets of a FISA-authorized phone tap were forced to appear in court because they called someone under surveillance. In 1988, after Vernon Bellecourt, Bill Means, and Bob Brown phoned a member of the Peoples' Committee for Libyan Students, they were forced to testify before a grand jury investigating the group. They were cited for contempt when they refused to testify.

The government obtained 20 separate FISA authorizations for surveillance while investigating Theresa M. Squillacote and Kurt A. Stand, who were convicted in 1998 of conspiring to commit espionage. The U.S. Supreme Court dismissed a petition filed for their attorneys to see the FISA documents justifying surveillance. The government claimed: "All required procedures were followed at all times...access to the FISA applications by the defendants' attorneys was correctly denied on national security grounds..."

In the case of Richard Johnson, the judge insisted to the jury that evidence against Johnson existed but wouldn't be presented for "national security." The evidence couldn't be challenged and the jury was to rely on the judge's testimony.

Samih Jammal, charged with running a ring to steal and resell baby formula, had been sending money to the Middle East and recruiting Middle Easterners in order for them to get immigration papers. Hardly a "national security" threat, Jammal was spied on under the FISA, and unable to learn why he was labeled a foreign agent engaged in espionage.

The "Portland Seven"

In a high-profile 2003 case, *United States v. Battle et. al.*, an Oregon federal court convicted seven Americans charged with conspiring to wage war against the U.S. and attempting to support the Taliban. They were also charged with weapons possession. They were accused of conspiring to help al-Qaeda, but the charge was dropped. The seven were mostly black American converted to Islam and the government claimed they constituted a terrorist cell.

Allegedly, some of those charged attempted to travel to Afghanistan in 2001, to help the Taliban and fellow Muslims fight American forces there. But the men never made it to Afghanistan. They got refused entry into Pakistan from China.

October Martinique Lewis was convicted for remaining in Portland and wiring money to Battle, her ex-husband.

Only the government knows why these people were targeted for surveillance. The FBI obtained FISA warrants to wiretap their phones, read their e-mail, and entered their homes, planting microphones. The bugging devices remained for months and intercepted more than 271 conversations, including those of children and visitors.

After learning of their FISA status, the defendants tried to review the FBI's FISC applications. Without knowing the basis for these "warrants," they couldn't know if their Fourth Amendment rights were violated, and that the government should reveal why the FBI targeted them, they argued.

They claimed that they were not "agents of a foreign power," that the government's secret court process was illegal, and that they were not engaged in international terrorism.

The American Civil Liberties Union agreed, and along with the National Association of Criminal Defense Lawyers, filed suit with the Supreme Court. The legal papers show that FISA was used to put the Portland Seven under surveillance, though its real purpose was to prosecute.

Before the PATRIOT Act, wiretaps could only be used to gather foreign intelligence, not to collect evidence for prosecution. The ACLU noted that restrictions on government surveillance that the UPA erased had been enacted after past abuses, urging the Portland federal district court to suppress the secret evidence. The Supreme Court refused to review the ACLU's case.

"The government's actions sound an ominous note for the future of privacy in America, in which the Constitution and the courts are treated like an obstacle, rather than a path, to justice," said Ann Beeson of the ACLU. "No one is questioning the government's authority to prosecute spies and terrorists, but we do not need to waive the Constitution in order to do so."

Without the evidence, the Portlanders were coerced by prosecutors into pleading guilty to "conspiring to wage war against the U.S." Oregon's First Assistant U.S. Attorney said the forced plea-offer was to avoid "difficult" challenges to the UPA.

Prosecutors resisted disclosure, and Ashcroft allowed only U.S. District Judge Robert Jones to review the FISA materials in secret and rule whether the FISA requests were justified. Many bewailed the outcome. "The concept of an independent judiciary...has been severely eroded if not completely dissipated," said the attorney representing Lewis. Were FISA warrants sought instead of normal warrants just because it was easier?

Law enforcement would have had trouble obtaining a regular criminal search warrant against this group of Americans. Evidence suggests that the only time Ahmed and Muhammad Bilal, the brothers involved, had ever shot a gun was during a target practice at an Oregon rock quarry. They never reached Pakistan, much less Afghanistan, never received training, and never fought a member of the U.S. military.

Ashcroft was right in stating that the arrests of those involved marked "a defining day in America's war against terrorism." The case set a precedent that U.S. citizens could be convicted of crimes without ever knowing why the government was allowed to spy on them in the first place.

The USA PATRIOT Act

USA PATRIOT Act stands for "Uniting and Strengthening America by Providing Appropriate Tools Required to Intercept and Obstruct Terrorism." After Sept. 11, 2001, Congress scrambled to pass legislation to prevent future attacks. Rushed into law six weeks after the WTC and Pentagon bombings, many congressmen admitted that they had not had time to read it. The UPA broke down barriers between intelligence and law enforcement. UPA eroded the concept that the primary purpose of spying was to investigate foreign intelligence.

The UPA had been written before 9/11 and Congress rejected Ashcroft's first UPA draft, which would have changed "primary purpose" to "a purpose." Further doubts lingered when it was revealed that earlier in 2001, Paul Wolfowitz had published a report suggesting that "a terrorist attack on U.S. soil" would allow legislation like the PATRIOT act to be passed.

Criminal law enforcement agencies were then allowed to direct FISA surveillance's and investigations. In 2002, the Attorney General approved guidelines letting prosecutors "advise intelligence officials on the initiation, operation, continuation, or expansion of FISA searches or surveillance." The Bush Administration claims that the UPA destroyed the wall between counterintelligence and criminal investigations. But FISA was clear about preserving this separation. Prosecutors collecting evidence in the name of "national security" is what the FISA was created to prevent.

When Bush signed the UPA into law, the crime of "domestic terrorism" was created. Vague enough that it could apply to acts of civil disobedience protected under the First Amendment, the UPA gives the FBI and the CIA greater rights to wiretap phones; monitor e-mail and internet use; survey medical, financial, and student records; break into homes and offices without notification; monitor purchases and library records; and add DNA samples to databases. In addition, the UPA makes it a crime for a librarian to inform someone that they are a FISA target.

The UPA provides for greater use of National Security Letters (NSLs), secret subpoenas, issued by the FBI, that demand records and information on people. The government does not need court approval to issue NSLs, and recipients cannot challenge them in court. Anyone who receives an NSL is "gagged" from telling anyone about it. Before the PATRIOT Act, the FBI could only use NSLs to get records on suspected terrorists and spies. Now NSLs can demand information about anyone at all.

According to official reports in 2005, 9,254 NSLs were sent to secretly get information on 3,501 U.S. citizens.

Illegal Use of the FISA

On May 17, 2002, the FISC refused to approve activities proposed by Ashcroft, claiming they were "not consistent with current federal law." This landmark was the first time the FISC had denied a request for FISA surveillance. Normally, FISC surveillance orders are reviewed and decided by one judge. However, the Court's opposition was so strong that the denial was signed by all 10 judges serving on the court and former presiding judge, Royce Lamberth.

The refused application had proposed electronic surveillance ostensibly to monitor an American's "terrorist network." The government had been conducting parallel and overlapping investigations of that person, using two separate law enforcement agencies in separate departments. The DOJ claimed the U.S. citizen was believed to be "aiding, abetting, or conspiring with others in international terrorism."

Details about the citizen are classified but the judges perceived the makings of a conspiracy between the police and intelligence, and required a chaperone to attend consultations and coordination between the two sides.

The FISC most objected to the allowing of law enforcement and prosecutors to direct intelligence officials, explaining, "such extensive collaboration would amount to law enforcement directing FISA surveillances and searches from start to finish, which it considers illegal." The Court explained that this amounted to using FISA to violate FISA. The FISC continued that FISA cannot "be used primarily for a law enforcement purpose." This was the first ruling against the PATRIOT Act.

"The secret court finally went public. In doing so, it exposed Attorney General John Ashcroft's efforts to use intelligence powers to circumvent the Constitution," said Gregory T. Nojeim, of the ACLU. "This strong opinion from the intelligence court proves once again that in this country, when the government is investigating crime, it must be able to show a judge strong evidence of wrongdoing before it is allowed to search a home or record telephone conversations." But the headlines were more shocking when they indicated that FBI agents had repeatedly and consistently lied when requesting and using permission for FISA surveillance.

"Mistakes," Secrets, and Lies

Starting around 2000, the FISC found that in more than 75 cases, the FBI had lied in its surveillance applications. FBI Supervisory Special Agent Michael Resnick pattern of lying so angered the Court that the FISC barred the agent from presenting surveillance applications.

Judges said that authorities had "improperly shared intelligence information with agents and prosecutors handling criminal cases in New York on at least four occasions." The Court concluded that the DOJ and New York law enforcement had conspired multiple times in illegal attempts to prosecute or imprison American citizens.

In most cases FISA targets have not committed crimes. If they had, law enforcement could use typical methods of probable cause to get warrants. Only about a dozen of the approximately 1,200 persons detained after 9/11 turned out to be terrorists. If we assume similar proportions apply to FISA targets, and only 1% of those under surveillance represent valid "national security" threats, then we are waging an expensive war against the political affiliations of mostly innocent people.

Now that the DOJ and law enforcement can legally conspire to imprison political enemies, it is also easy for them to fabricate physical evidence. They can tamper with your belongings, to produce whatever "evidence" is needed.

If the FBI would lie and falsify evidence, claiming "national security" status when they can't get a regular warrant, how could they be trusted with more power through

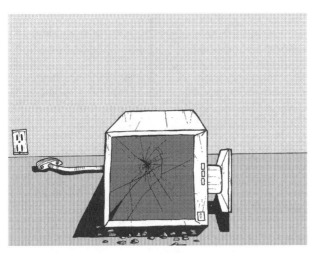

FISA? FBI Director Louis Freeh lied to the FISC under oath. He claimed that a target was not already being investigated by law enforcement, when the target was. FBI agents illegally shared classified material with law enforcement and prosecutors and colluded with them. Agents knowingly swore to false statements that they had not already been investigating a FISA target, when they actually had. The Court complained of "erroneous statements" and "omissions of material facts."

But the problems weren't limited to FISA applications. Distraught FBI agents complained about "mistakes" during the act of surveillance, including: videotaping a meeting without authorization, continuing to read a target's email without authorization, and continuing to wiretap a cell phone after the phone number had changed to a new subscriber.

Unauthorized searches, incorrect addresses, incorrect interpretations of FISA orders, and other problems continued. FBI software picked up emails of not only a target but of others as well. In a case where a "wall" had supposedly existed between intelligence and criminal squads, it turned out that "all of the FBI agents were on the same squad and all of the screening was done by the one supervisor overseeing both investigations." A letter from the FBI's Counterterrorism Division notes that "errors" grew by three-and-one-half times from the year 1999 to the year 2000.

An FBI agent's letter concludes, "You have a pattern of occurrences which indicate...an inability on the part of the FBI to manage its FISAs."

The Court noted this, saying, "in an alarming number of instances, there have been troubling results" regarding lies in FISA applications, noting a "troubling number of inaccurate FBI affidavits in so many FISA applications." Intelligence agents had repeatedly violated the Court's orders. "How these misrepresentations occurred remains unexplained to the court," the FISC stated.

When this became public, Lawrence Goldman, President of the National Association of Criminal Defense Lawyers, stated: "It is no surprise to criminal defense lawyers that warrant applications by law enforcement authorities often contain misleading and even false statements. It is particularly disturbing, and surprising, that even the director of the FBI presented false information to the FISA court... If the federal authorities have confessed to 75 instances of misleading this one court of limited jurisdiction, the number of times they have misled other courts must be well into the thousands... This latest revelation shows us that the courts cannot accept blindly the assertions of government officials."

The FISC learned of many of these lies and violations only because FBI and DOJ employees were troubled by the massive corruption and came forward.

Bad Grades for the FBI

In 2003, Senate Judiciary Committee Members Leahy, Grassley, and Specter's report was the first comprehensive oversight of the FBI in almost 20 years.

The senators said: "[FBI] Headquarters' role is to know the law and 'connect the dots' from multiple sources...The FBI failed in this." They noted: "the bureaucratic hurdles erected by Headquarters (and DOJ)...contributed to inaccurate information being presented to the FISA Court, eroding the trust in the FBI..."

They pointed to excess secrecy: "This secrecy has been extended to the most basic legal and procedural aspects of the FISA, which should not be secret. This unnecessary secrecy contributed to the deficiencies..." The DOJ and FBI had refused to answer questions regarding even unclassified matters.

The DOJ and FBI don't seem to want anyone—even Congress—to know what they are doing with FISA and UPA. The senators complain in their report: "We are disappointed with the non-responsiveness of the DOJ and FBI...Often, legitimate requests went unanswered or the DOJ answers were delayed for so long or were so incomplete that they were of minimal use...The difficulty in obtaining responses from DOJ prompted Senator Specter to ask the Attorney General directly, 'How do we communicate with you and are you really too busy to respond?'"

But there were other problems. "A deep-rooted culture of ignoring problems and discouraging employees from criticizing the FBI contributes to the FBI's repetition of its past mistakes in the foreign intelligence field. There has been little or no progress at the FBI in addressing this culture..."

More cultural problems included "the FBI's 'circle the wagons' mentality, wherein those who report flaws in the FBI are punished for their frankness; and the FBI's flawed internal disciplinary procedures and 'double standard' in discipline, in which line FBI agents can be seriously punished for the same misconduct that only earns senior FBI executives a slap on the wrist."

Alarmingly, the senators noted that a hearing in 2002 "exposed a deep-seated cultural bias against the importance of security at the FBI" and "the highly inappropriate handling of sensitive FISA materials...massive amounts of the most sensitive and highly classified materials in the FBI's possession were made available on an unrestricted basis to nearly all FBI employees. Even more disturbing, this action was taken without proper consultation with the FBI's own security officials."

On FISA surveillance, the senators note: "These types of investigations give rise to a tension between the government's legitimate national security interests...and... constitutional safeguards against unreasonable government searches and seizures and excessive government intrusion into the exercise of free speech, associational, and privacy rights...winning the war on terrorism would be a hollow victory indeed if it came only at the cost of the very liberties we are fighting to preserve."

"Passage of the USA PATRIOT Act," they wryly continue, "did not solve the longstanding and acknowledged problems at the FBI."

The senators conclude: "Indeed, in many ways the DOJ and FBI's shortcomings in implementing the FISA...present a compelling case for both comprehensive FBI reform and close congressional oversight and scrutiny." Unfortunately, "Oversight of the entire FISA process is hampered...because the Congress and the public get no access to any work of the FISA Court, even work that is unclassified. This secrecy is unnecessary, and allows problems in applying the law to fester."

"Many things are different now since the tragic events of [9/11], but one thing that has not changed is the United States Constitution. Congress must work to guarantee the civil liberties of our people while at the same time meet our obligations to America's national security. Excessive secrecy and unilateral decision making by a single branch of government is not the proper method of striking that all important balance..."

DOJ's Appeal

Despite criticisms, the Justice Department appealed the FISA Court's rejection of its 2002 application for surveillance. The appeal was heard by the FISA Court of Review, and marked the first time in history that this three-judge court convened.

Unlike regular appeal courts, the FISA Court of Review only hears arguments and evidence from the government. No one argued for the lower FISA court's position. The DOJ was even allowed to present the review court with an argument it had not used at the lower FISA court.

The law professor Turley says, "To call this a court of appeals is to stretch the conventional definition of an appeals process...In a real court of appeals you would have a collection of opposing views. You would also have an argument that would occur in public so citizens could judge the merits of the government's position."

Defending the FISA, Ashcroft used the "end justifies the means" argument, saying: "it is the nature of the threat, not the nature of the government's response to that threat, which determines the constitutionality of FISA searches and surveillance." He placed the rights of government above the rights of citizens by saying, "Although 'foreign intelligence information' must be relevant or necessary to 'protect' against the specified threats, the statutory definition does not limit how the government may use the information to achieve that protection."

Ashcroft claims that someone can be labeled an "agent of a foreign power" if such a designation is necessary for the government to get a FISA surveillance order and attempt to prosecute that person or otherwise violate his or her liberties and that the government should be able to commit illegal or unconstitutional acts if it feels itself threatened in any way.

However, with no one allowed to present an opposing view, Ashcroft and the DOJ won the case.

The appeals court stated that it was not ready to "jettison Fourth Amendment requirements in the interest of national security," but admitted that FISA orders violate the Fourth Amendment. Weakly, it concluded: "we think the procedures and government showings required under FISA, if they do not meet the minimum Fourth Amendment warrant standards, certainly come close."

After the verdict, the ACLU filed suit with the Supreme Court. But the high court dismissed the appeal on a technicality.

Warrantless Wiretapping, Bush, and the NSA

Around this time, President Bush took a different approach. He decided to ditch the courts, and secretly authorized the NSA to eavesdrop on Americans inside the U.S.—bypassing the FISA. After sitting on the story for a year, *The New York Times* broke the news that, since 2002, the NSA has domestically monitored the phone calls and internet communications of thousands of people, without obtaining warrants.

It was FBI officials who complained about the NSA program, believing it violated the rights of law-abiding citizens. According to *The New York Times*, FBI Director

Mueller even raised concerns about the program's legality.

Contrary to initial claims, the surveillance program monitored domestic communications, not just international calls. "This is really a sea change," said a former national security official. "It's almost a mainstay of this country that the NSA only does foreign searches." The *Washington Post* reported "fewer than 10 U.S. citizens or residents a year...have aroused enough suspicion during warrantless eavesdropping to justify interception of their domestic calls."

In the first landmark case, Greenpeace award-winning author James Bamford and the ACLU jointly sued the NSA for monitoring them. A federal judge found that the president had personally violated the First Amendment, Fourth Amendment, and FISA.

By violating the FISA, President Bush has committed a felony but vowed to continue the program, undaunted.

Various sources observe that the NSA is not only targeting individuals, but using broad "data mining" systems domestically. Via satellite, the NSA monitors every call, fax, email, telex, and computer data message. It then programs specific keywords into computers to sift through all this information in the hunt for specific profiles.

The results are what you might expect. According to *The New York Times*, the NSA has sent the FBI masses of information. But the information was largely useless. One former FBI agent said, "We'd chase a number, find it's a schoolteacher with no indication they've ever been involved in international terrorism." For government agencies, this can seem trivial or a waste of time. But for innocent citizens, this is a violation of privacy.

Eventually AT&T was found to be in violation of the law by assisting in this illegal surveillance and President Obama campaigned on holding AT&T accountable for breaking these laws and providing information about law-abiding U.S. citizens to the DOJ and FBI. But after winning the election, Obama went back against his campaign promise and supported Bush's bill that would allow amnesty for AT&T and condoned the illegal wiretapping through the FISA Amendments Act of 2008.

The Bush administration avoided any of their own convictions of wrong doing by shrouding the eavesdropping in such utter secrecy that nobody could prove they were a target or that their privacy had been compromised. As a result, no one had standing to contest the legality of the NSA's actions.

Eye in the Sky

Since Sept. 11, 2001, Defense Department employees at the National Geospatial-Intelligence Agency have used sophisticated technology to watch most every inch of the U.S. This technology can depict objects or activities anywhere on Earth and from space, it can view objects just inches long.

If the information is linked to "national security," the NGS may target a specific individual—and highlight a suspect's home. Government agencies are increasingly using satellites to keep tabs on possible enemies.

A claim by office director Bert Beaulieu that the NGS "couldn't care less about [spying on] individuals and people and companies" doesn't wash with secrecy expert Steven Aftergood, who says, "What it all boils down to is, 'Trust us. Our intentions are good.'"

U.S. exploitation of satellite technology has been developing for many years, expanding into "economic espionage." During the Clinton administration, the European Union was aghast to find evidence indicating that the U.S., Britain, and other countries had been using the "Echelon" satellite system to get the upper hand on European companies in financial deals.

Americans' privacy concerns, however, are closer to home. When a court denied a DOJ request to monitor a cell phone's location, the public learned that the DOJ has already been tracking cell phone users' movements—without probable cause or legal authority.

Beginning in 2005, the State Department has reportedly been placing RFID chips in all U.S. passports with plans to place chips in many states' drivers' licenses.

Secret Military Tribunals

Because of the emergency presented by the events of September 11, 2001, President Bush decreed the creation of secret military tribunals for foreigners whom the President claims he has "reason to believe" are members of terrorist organizations.

Little has been revealed about the practices of these clandestine panels. President Bush granted himself and the Secretary of Defense exclusive power to create the tribunals, appoint their officers, make their laws, and expand their own powers. The courts meet secretly, withhold evidence under "national security," exclude defendants from their own trials, allow the prosecution to admit hearsay and coerced evidence, find a defendant guilty even if a third of the officers disagreed, and execute the accused, who can not appeal to any other court.

In 2006, the Supreme Court struck down the use of these tribunals, saying they violated the Constitution and international law. The court found that Bush had neither the authority nor a reason for this type of military trial.

"It would be unacceptable...in my opinion, to give someone the death penalty in a trial where they never heard the evidence against them," said Senator Lindsey Graham of South Carolina. "'Trust us, you're guilty, we're going to execute you, but we can't tell you why.'"

The tribunals are supposedly only used against foreigners whom the government suspects of ties to terrorism, but secret military tribunals are used in tandem by the government against Americans. The most famous case of which was probably that of Bradley Manning, a private suspected of communicating information about U.S. war crimes to the website WikiLeaks. He was held in extended solitary confinement before being put on trial without representation or any real hope of a fair trial or appeal. Manning faces 22 charges related to the alleged leak of hundreds of thousands of documents to WikiLeaks and stands to face life in prison for his whistleblowing.

In 2006 seven members of Stop Huntington Animal Cruelty were prosecuted as terrorists under secret courts under the controversial Animal Enterprise Protection Act, which allows domestic dissidents to be charged as terrorists. The case boiled down to a conviction for setting up a webpage that directed others on how to work to challenge Huntington's Life Sciences animal testing lab. Because the labs are in both England and New Jersey, the "SHAC-7" were convicted of "conspiracy to commit interstate stalking" as part of a "global conspiracy."

A President's inner circle can secretly spy on, convict, torture, and/or execute Americans whom government officials do not like. It is the vision of what James Madison called "tyranny."

According to John Ashcroft, expressing a dissenting viewpoint makes you an "agent of a foreign power," and criticizing the government was "aiding the terrorists."

In a recent case of an exposed small stakes gambling ring in Seattle, Detective Bryan Van Brunt, the police's agent provocateur, spent two years and at least tens of thousands of dollars in an attempt to convict crimes, expecting politically-motivated actions from the poker players. And by the end, the undercover officer was funding and encouraging their involvement in political activities that they weren't all that interested in, but were encouraged to participate in, out of loyalty to their friend, who had covered even their rents and travel expenses. The agent had pushed prosecuted individuals into things they never would have done on their own and in the end there still weren't many crimes to prosecute.

In England, the situation is even stranger. Undercover police infiltrate activist groups and will carry the charade so far that the officers testify under their fake identity in court and get sentenced along with actual participants. And similar to environmental activist Eric McDavid's case in the U.S., an undercover officer in London, Andrew James Boyling, ended up marrying one of his marks.

Beginning around 1995, Boyling was sent to infiltrate saboteur campaigners. Masquerading as an activist, he joined the group Reclaim The Streets, who took over public roads and staged imaginative parties in protest of the domination of cars. Boyling quickly became a trusted member of the campaign, showing up at weekly meetings and protests.

"He was totally deeply embedded in the whole social network as well. Meetings often happened in the top room of a pub so he would be there and end up living with people," said an activist from the group.

Boyling was among a group of protesters who occupied the office of the chairman of London Transport and were arrested in 1996. Lawyers for the defendants pieced together how far the deception went. According to another participant, "the undercover officer played a major role in initiating conduct which was then prosecuted."

Once arrested, Boyling was taken to Charing Cross police station, there he declared he was "Peter James Sutton," and gave a false date of birth. Being prosecuted in court bolstered Boyling's position in the group and by 1999 he was trusted by their inner core. That same year, he seemed to develop actual feelings of love for a Reclaim The Streets activist and moved in with her.

Suddenly he left in September 2000, saying that he was going to Turkey and South Africa.

The War Is On

Grand juries, despite being of dubious constitutionality, are relied upon in these cases to force testimony from people who may have information that could be used to convict others. They are typically utilized in cases of politically sensitive activity and recent cases have involved charges of "racketeering" for suggesting that others should read books that encourage seditious activities and lifestyles. Refusing to testify to a grand jury is, itself, a felony and those who refuse to testify can be held for as long as the judge deems it possible that they may testify in the future.

President Obama, despite his branding as a progressive liberal, has continued to crack down on activists, erode constitutionally protected rights to privacy, and give himself increasingly unrestrained surveillance authority. He endorsed and pushed for the FISA Amendments Act—and an extension of it until 2017—that allows the federal government to maintain a gigantic electronic surveillance dragnet to grab, store, and search the public's personal telephone calls, emails, internet activites, and other private activities without a search warrant or even proof that the information was gathered because of suspicion of any particular crime or conspiracy. Obama campaigned on and continually promised FISA reform but has instead strengthened the network in Bush's footsteps.

The Obama DOJ has used similar methods to the Bush DOJ, saying essentially: If you can't prove that we are spying on you illegally, because we are so secretive about who we are actually spying on, then you have no case against us. So far, this absurd argument initially created by the Bush administration has been upheld.

Conclusion

Our current erosion of liberties is the product of a long-standing struggle that has existed since our country began.

American revolutionaries rebelled against the power-hungry King of England's practice of taxation, excessive monitoring, torture, and imprisonment. During America's eugenics movement, arrogant, aristocratic government employees monitored, physically violated, and imprisoned citizens. The paranoid 1960s and Nixon years brought unlawful monitoring, imprisonment, harassment, and murders of protesters. We are now in the most recent wave of monitoring, harassment, imprisonment, and torture—at the same time that we are seeing an unprecedented expansion of presidential power and murdering drones.

The past decade has shown us the danger of unchecked expansion. In the neo-con era, the balance has tilted from protecting Americans to assaulting anyone who is disliked by members of the President's cabal. Eroticism has been replaced by violence.

Old-World tradition has oppressed our history, and spurred America's social revolutions—the birth struggles of the New World. Government behaves less like a monolithic, protective entity, and more like a self-defensive, paranoid, and precarious collection of factions with personal agendas—with a history of genocide.

Further Reading and Sources

ACLU v. NSA, 06-CV-10204 (E.D. Mich. 2006)

ACLU.org. "Government is Illegally Using Evidence from Secret Court Wiretaps in Criminal Cases, ACLU Charges." 9/19/03.

ACLU.org. "Secret Wiretap Court Exposes Ashcroft Plans to Circumvent the Constitution." 9/23/02.

Aftergood, Steven. "Foreign Intelligence Surveillance Court Opens Up." Secrecy News, from the FAS (Federation of American Scientists) Project on Government Secrecy Vol. 2002, No. 83, 8/27/02.

Aftergood, Steven. "Supreme Court Rebuffs FISA Challenge." Secrecy News (from the FAS Project on Government Secrecy), 4/23/01.

American Civil Liberties Union. "The Dangers of Domestic Spying by Federal Law Enforcement: A Case Study of FBI Surveillance of Dr. Martin Luther King."

American Philosophical Society. Eugenics Record Office Records. www.amphilsoc. org/library/mole/e/ero.htm.

Aris, Ben; Campbell, Duncan. "How Bush's Grandfather Helped Hitler's Rise to Power." *The Guardian*, 9/25/04.

Associated Press. "Bush to Unveil Plan for Guantanamo Trials." *The New York Times*, 9/6/06.

Bamford, James. *Body of Secrets: Anatomy of the Ultra-Secret National Security Agency*. Random House, 2001.

Barrett v. United States, 798 F.2d 565 (2nd Cir. 1986).

Bergman, Lowell; Lichtblau, Eric; Shane, Scott; Van Natta, Don; Rashbaum, William K. "Domestic Surveillance: The Program; Spy Agency Data after Sept. 11 led F.B.I. to Dead Ends," *The New York Times*, 1/17/06, A1.

Bordc.org (Bill of Rights Defense Committee website).

Bruinius, Harry. *Better for All the World: The Secret History of Forced Sterilization and America's Quest for Racial Purity*. Alfred A. Knopf, 2006.

Bryant, Daniel. (from a letter by Assistant Attorney General Daniel Bryant to members of the Select Committee on Intelligence). U.S. Department of Justice, 7/31/02.

Buck v. Bell, 274 U.S. 200 (1927)

Budnick, Nick. "John Ashcroft's Close Call The Portland Seven Case Avoids A Legal Challenge To The Patriot Act." *Willamette Week*, 10/23/03.

Carlson, Elof Axel. *The Unfit: A History of a Bad Idea*. Cold Spring Harbor Laboratory Press, 2001.

Clinton, William J. "Remarks by President William J. Clinton in Acceptance of Human Radiation Final Report," October 3, 1995.

Clinton, William J. "Executive Order 12891—Advisory Committee on Human Radiation Experiments," 59 Fed. Reg. 13 (January 20, 1994).

Clinton, William J. Memorandum of March 27, 1997—Strengthened Protections for Human Subjects of Classified Research.

Colangelo, Philip. "The Secret FISA Court: Rubber Stamping On Rights." *Albion Monitor* (reprinted by permission from *Covert Action Quarterly*). 10/30/95.

Daley, Suzanne. "An Electronic Spy Scare Is Alarming Europe." *The New York Times*, 2/24/00.

Democracy Now! "An Impeachable Offense: Bush Admits Authorizing NSA to Eavesdrop on Americans Without Court Approval." Transcript, 12/19/05.

Department of Justice (John Ashcroft et. al.). "Brief for the United States on Appeal from the United States Foreign Intelligence Surveillance Court."

Eff.org (Electronic Frontier Foundation).

Eggen, Dan; Schmidt, Susan. "Secret Court Rebuffs Ashcroft: Justice Dept. Chided on Misinformation." *Washington Post*, 8/23/02, A1.

Encyclopedia.com

Epic.org. "ABA Urges FISA Oversight." The Electronic Privacy Information Center (EPIC), 2/12/03.

Federation of American Scientists, The (FAS). Secrecy & Government Bulletin, 9/95.

Final Report of the Select Committee to Study Governmental Operations with Respect to Intelligence Activities of the United States Senate (Church Committee Report), 94th Congress, 2nd Session, 1976.

FoxNews.com. "ACLU Sues Feds Over FISA Court." 2/19/03.

FoxNews.com. "FISA Court Weighs Handing More Power to Justice." 9/10/02.

GlobalSecurity.com

Grigg, William Norman. "Terror Tribunals."

In Re Cincinnati Radiation Litigation, 874 F. Supp. 796 (S.D. Ohio 1995)

Kevles, Daniel J. *In the Name of Eugenics: Genetics and the Uses of Human Heredity*. Harvard University Press, 1985.

Kuhl, Stefan. *The Nazi Connection: Eugenics, American Racism, and German National Socialism*. Oxford University Press, 1994.

Larabee, Mark. "Ashcroft: Portland Case Needs Secrecy." *The Oregonian*, 9/12/03.

Leahy, Senator Patrick; Grassley, Senator Charles; Specter, Senator Arlen. "Interim Report on FBI Oversight in the 107th Congress by the Senate Judiciary Committee: FISA Implementation Failures." 2/03.

Levendosky, Charles. "Secret Review Court Broadens Secret Searches." *Casper Star-Tribune*, 11/24/02.

Lindlaw, Scott. "U.S. Mulls Military's Domestic Role." Associated Press.

Liptak, Adam; Lichtblau, Eric. "U.S. Judge Finds Wiretap Actions Violate the Law." *The New York Times*, 8/18/06.

Lithwick, Dahlia. "Secrets And Lies: 75 Little Reasons To Be Afraid Of The FISA Court." www.slate.com.

Lumpkin, Beverley. "FISA Court Speaks, And Justice Objects."ABCNews.com.

McCullagh, Declan. "American Bar Association Urges More Oversight of FISA Court." Politech, 2/13/03.

McCullagh, Declan. "Snooping by Satellite." CNETNews.com, 1/12/05.

National Association of Criminal Defense Lawyers. "FISA Court and FBI." 9/23/02.

The Nose. *Willamette Week*, 9/03.

NSAWatch.org.

Office of the U.S. Attorney General. Annual Reports on the Foreign Intelligence Surveillance Court. 1979-2003.

Poole, Patrick. "ECHELON: America's Secret Global Surveillance Network." 1999/2000.

Ramasastry, Anita. "Why The Foreign Intelligence Surveillance Act Court Was Right To Rebuke The Justice Department." FindLaw's Writ, 9/4/02.

Ridley, Matt. Genome: The Autobiography of a Species in 23 Chapters. HarperCollins, 1999.

Risen, James; Lichtblau, Eric. "Bush Secretly Lifted Some Limits on Spying in U.S. After 9/11, Officials Say." *The New York Times*, 12/15/05.

Risen, James; Lichtblau, Eric. "Spying Program Snared U.S. Calls." *The New York Times*, 2/21/05.

Roberts, Dorothy. *Killing the Black Body: Race, Reproduction, and the Meaning of Liberty*. Vintage Books, 1997.

Safire, William. "Seizing Dictatorial Power." *The New York Times*, 2001.

Sanger, David E. "A Challenge from Bush to Congress." *The New York Times*, 9/7/06.

"Secret Court Rebuffs Ashcroft: Justice Dept. Chided on Misinformation." *Washington Post*, 8/23/02, A1.

Shenon, Philip. "Secret Court Says F.B.I. Aides Misled Judges in 75 Cases." *The New York Times*, 8/23/02.

Shrader, Katherine Pfleger. "Spy Imagery Watching Inside U.S." Associated Press/ *USA Today*, 9/26/04.

Stout, David. "Appeals Panel Reverses Limits Placed on Justice Dept. Wiretaps." *The New York Times*, 11/18/02.

TalkLeft. 9/402

Tietz, Jeff. "The Unending Torture of Omar Khadr." *Rolling Stone*, 8/24/06.

Tucker, William H. *The Funding of Scientific Racism: Wickliffe Draper and the Pioneer Fund*. University of Illinois Press, 2002.

U.S. Department of Justice. Foreign Intelligence Surveillance Act 2005 Annual Report.

U.S. Department of Justice. Responses to Questions from Chairman Sensenbrenner. 3/24/06.

Van Bergen, Jennifer. "Conyers Condemns Today's FISA..." TruthOut.org.

Van Bergen, Jennifer. "Secret Court Decision Silently Overrules Provision of PATRIOT Act." Truthout.org, 8/25/02.

Wolf, Paul. "FISA Court Decision." Federation of American Scientists, 9/2/02.

Zanoni, Mary. "Let Those Who Have Ears Listen Very, Very Closely: USDA and State Agency Doublespeak on Mandatory Animal HD."

Zernike, Kate. "Lawyers and G.O.P. Chiefs Resist Proposal on Tribunal." *The New York Times*, 9/8/06

The CIA Makes
Fiction Unex

The FBI
assassination of
Puerto Rican
independence leader
Filiberto Ojeda Rios

Chapter 4

Friday, September 23, 2005—The FBI fired over 120 bullets into the home of Puerto Rican independence leader Filiberto Ojeda Rios. They waited to enter his home for over 20 hours; by which time he had bled to death from unattended wounds. Autopsy reports show that his death was a result of bleeding out from a gunshot wound to his shoulder.

The FBI considered Ojeda Rios the head of a domestic terrorist group—the militant Puerto Rican independence group "Los Macheteros." But in Puerto Rico he has long been viewed as a leader of the independence movement. Many see him as a martyr who was killed at the hands of U.S. agents. And Puerto Ricans of all political stripes have questioned the FBI's actions, especially because the shooting took place on the anniversary of an 1868 uprising against imposed Spanish rule.

Puerto Rico is illegally occupied by the U.S. and under international law, the actions of the U.S. are terrorism and the Puerto Ricans are freedom fighters. At the time, the killing sparked an outpouring of anti-U.S. sentiment in Puerto Rico and fear that the Bush administration would launch a new crackdown on the remainder of the Puerto Rican independence movement.

Tens of thousands attended Rios' funeral—making it one of the largest in Puerto Rican history. Puerto Rican officials, 3 U.S. senators, and Amnesty International have called for an independent probe into his assassination. Amnesty said that the killing should be considered an extra-judicial execution if the FBI deliberately killed Ojeda Rios or deliberately left him to die, when they could have arrested him. The FBI claimed they were responding to 15 year old charges that Ojeda Rios was involved in a U.S. bank robbery.

Spanish Occupation of Puerto Rico

Situated in the northeast of the Caribbean Sea, Puerto Rico was key to the Spanish Empire from the beginning of its conquest and colonization of the New World. The smallest of the Greater Antilles, Puerto Rico was a major military post during many wars between Spain and the other European powers for control of the region during the 17th and 18th centuries. It was a quick stopover from Europe to Cuba, Mexico,

Central America, or the northern territories of South America. Through most of the 19th century, Puerto Rico and Cuba remained the last two Spanish colonies in the New World, and served as the final outposts in Spanish plans to regain control of the American continent.

By the early 1860s, Spanish authorities, alarmed by discovering plans from separatist groups, used severe measures against dissidents in Puerto Rico. Freedom of the press was non-existent and group discussions were monitored by the government.

By 1867, Puerto Rico had established a sense of national culture, represented in music, arts, colloquial language, and architecture. The majority of Puerto Ricans lived in extreme poverty while agriculture—the main source of income—was impeded by a lack of roads, insufficient tools and equipment, hurricanes, and drought. Despite an illiteracy rate of 83.7%, the citizens remained relatively active within the limitations imposed by local Spanish authorities.

Supporters of Puerto Rican independence and others who called for basic reforms under Spain were jailed or exiled during this period. At the same time, the island suffered a severe economic crisis from increasing tariffs and taxes imposed by Spain on import and export goods—the Spanish Crown badly needed these funds to subsidize its troops in an effort to regain control of the Dominican Republic.

Frustrated by the lack of political and economic freedom, and enraged by the continuing repression, an armed rebellion was staged by a pro-independence movement in 1868 called "Grito de Lares." Dr. Ramón Emeterio Betances and Segundo Ruiz Belvis founded the "Comité Revolucionario de Puerto Rico" (Revolutionary Committee of Puerto Rico) and led the group. Betances authored several "Proclamas" attacking the exploitation of the Puerto Ricans by the Spanish colonial system and called for immediate insurrection. These statements soon circulated throughout the island as local dissident groups began to organize. Secret cells of the Revolutionary Committee were established in Puerto Rico bringing together members from all sectors of society, to include landowners, merchants, professionals, peasants, and slaves. The critical state of the economy, along with the increasing repression, were the catalysts for rebellion. The movement was based in towns in the mountains of the western part of the island.

Poorly trained and armed, the rebels reached the town of Lares by horse and foot. They looted local stores and offices owned by "peninsulares" (Spanish-born men) and took over city hall, proclaiming the new Republic of Puerto Rico. Spanish merchants and local government authorities, considered by the rebels to be enemies of the fatherland, were taken as prisoners. The following day, the Republic of Puerto Rico was proclaimed under the presidency of Francisco Ramírez. All slaves that had joined the movement were declared free citizens. The rebel forces then departed to take over the next town, San Sebastián del Pepino. The Spanish militia, however, surprised the group with strong resistance, causing great confusion among the armed rebels who, led by Manuel Rojas, retreated back to Lares. Upon an order from the governor, Julián Pavía, the Spanish militia soon rounded up the rebels and quickly brought the insurrection to an end. Some 475 rebels were imprisoned, among them, Manuel Rojas. On November 17, a military court imposed the death penalty, for treason and sedition, on all prisoners.

After these events, the liberal faction of Puerto Rico called for it to become a true province of Spain, receiving the privileges of the then-liberal Spanish regime. The liberals called for the abolition of slavery and ample political reforms at the local level. In November 1870, the liberals founded the Partido Liberal Reformista (Liberal Reform Party). Unfortunately, the leadership was divided; half supported

total assimilation to Spain, while the "autonomistas" called for self-government under the Spanish flag. The newspaper *El Progreso* served as a vehicle for public expression of the liberals' views.

Despite political reforms, local Spanish authorities kept a tight grip on the island, threatened by rumors from abroad of plots and potential insurrection by the separatists. In this, censorship of the press was particularly effective as were government repression and political persecution directed at the liberal camp.

Between 1876 and 1898, both liberal wings came together under the idea of political autonomy, discarding assimilation with Spain. Puerto Ricans were finally granted self-government by Spain when the "Carta Autonómica" (constitutional autonomy) was approved by the Spanish Cortes in November 25, 1897. But by the time of the first elections in March 1898, tensions were building between Spain and the U.S. and the short-lived self-government experiment came to an abrupt end one month later with the advent of the Spanish-American War.

Of all the Spanish colonies in the Americas, Puerto Rico is the only territory that never gained independence. After four centuries of Spanish colonial rule, the period between 1860 and 1898 showed a pro-independence rebellion, colonial reform, the establishment of the first national political parties, the abolition of slavery, and a short-lived experiment in autonomy under Spanish rule. Spain's military and political power in the region was receding, and the U.S. was an emerging regional, imperialist power. This placed Puerto Rico, along with Cuba, as key territories in the Caribbean. This power imbalance culminated in the formal transfer of the island to the United States in 1898 after the Spanish-American War.

U.S. Occupation of Puerto Rico

The strategic value of Puerto Rico for the U.S. in 1898 stemmed from economic and military interests. The island's value to U.S. policy makers was as an outlet for excess manufactured goods, as well as a key naval station.

In 1896, a formal war plan was developed by Lieutenant William W. Kimball, a naval intelligence officer at the War College. The stated objective was to "liberate Cuba." The main theater of operations would be the Caribbean, focusing on the Cuban and Puerto Rican coastal regions, and the conflict would involve exclusively naval operations. Despite tactical and logistical faults, unquestionable military superiority over Spanish forces led to a quick U.S. victory.

The Spanish-American war lasted for 4 months. U.S. troops landed in Cuba late in June and on July 17 destroyed the Spanish fleet stationed in Santiago de Cuba Bay, securing control of the waterways in the Caribbean. President McKinley set forth the conditions for peace negotiations, including the transfer of Puerto Rico from Spanish authorities to the United States without compensation.

President McKinley's conditions for a peace agreement were ratified in the Treaty of Paris on December 10, 1898. The formal transfer took two months and the U.S. flag was raised in most public buildings on the island. A military government was established under the command of General John R. Brooke.

A sense of powerlessness and unpredictability in Puerto Rican life prevailed under U.S. rule. When Spanish colonial rule was replaced by that of the U.S., Maldonado Denis wrote, "The majority of the population—the peasants and workers— of course remained on the periphery, accepting the change of sovereignty with the same fatalism with which they accepted hookworm, hurricanes, and tuberculosis."

Puerto Rico remained under direct control of U.S. military forces until the U.S. Congress ratified the Foraker Law on April 12th, 1900, bringing a civilian government to the island. For over 100 years, the U.S. has held Puerto Rico in colonial status—with 13 military bases on the island to threaten the Caribbean and Latin America. This occupation of Puerto Rican land wrecked the agriculture of the island and has driven many to the cities of the United States. It also has given rise to constant resistance, including new and powerful movements for independence and national liberation. In the heat of the 1960s and 1970s, new organizations rose up to fight for Puerto Rican liberation— based both in the island itself and in the large Puerto Rican communities of U.S. cities.

Similarly to the Spanish, the U.S. government mobilized its agents to hunt down and prosecute members of these movements. These agents used any methods they could to suppress the Puerto Rican resistance, including: manufactured evidence, disinformation campaigns, agents, infiltrators, and all kinds of secret police surveillance. After their capture, these fighters were unjustly imprisoned, persecuted, and subjected to brutal torture within the U.S. prison system.

Almost instantly after takeover, a public school system was established by the U.S. to maintain imperialist and colonial ideology. The invaders instilled fear by means of terror and propagated the myth that if the U.S. were to "abandon" Puerto Rico, the people would die of hunger.

Spanish rule in Puerto Rico was strict and autocratic, and Puerto Rican natives were treated as inferior in every way. American officials continued that tradition after taking possession of the island. A contemporary observer wrote that the new American masters treated Puerto Ricans as though they "believed the Island sprung from the ocean just on the eve of the landing of American troops." For 30 years Puerto Rican school lessons were taught in English and the island's name was spelled as Porto Rico for the convenience of the non-Spanish colonizers.

The Puerto Rican sense of inferiority was reinforced by the U.S. policy decision to make the island an unincorporated territory. The civil rights of native Puerto Ricans were therefore not constitutionally guaranteed but congressionally determined. For 17 years the inhabitants of the island were officially called "The People of Puerto Rico" but were not citizens of any country. It was as if Puerto Ricans, as "natives" of an underdeveloped foreign land, were thought to be unworthy of U.S. citizenship. Congress did not confer U.S. citizenship on Puerto Ricans until 1917, but even then, the Jones Act which granted Puerto Ricans U.S. citizenship included provisions that curtailed the authority of the popularly-elected Puerto Rican legislature, and invested the U.S.-appointed governor of the island and the U.S. president with the power to veto any laws passed by the Puerto Rican legislature.

Puerto Rico was not allowed to have a constitution until 1952.

U.S. & FBI Harrassment

Even today there continues to be many reports of independentistas being dismissed from civil employment because of their political affiliation, media stations being denied broadcasting permits for providing regular airtime to independence groups, and passports being refused for independence leaders seeking to travel in South America. Independentistas have been threatened, bombed, or shot at— sometimes while the police stand by.

One of the first major U.S. government atrocities was the Ponce Massacre of February 1937, in the city of Ponce, Puerto Rico. The police surrounded and fired on a peaceful demonstration for the pro-independence Nationalist Party of Albizu Campos. Twenty civilians were killed, 150 were

wounded. On October 30, 1950, U.S. forces in Puerto Rico put down an uprising of 2,000 Nationalists. Two days later, two Nationalists, Oscar Collazo and Grisilio Torresola, tried unsuccessfully to assassinate President Harry Truman in Washington.

In 1954 the Nationalists led an attack on the U.S. Capitol building that wounded several legislators. A pamphlet by the Movement Pro Independence, *Time for Independence* in 1963 described the repression directed against the independence movement:

"The objective is to surround the fighters for independence, to isolate them from the rest of society. The repressive policy extends from economic pressure, press defamation, reprisals in business, professions and employment, to open and shameless police terror."

In response to the impact of the Cuban Revolution and the radicalization that was beginning to take place in Puerto Rico, the FBI initiated an operation in 1960 as part of its COINTELPRO program that targeted the Puerto Rican independence movement, both in Puerto Rico and within the U.S. The FBI had instructions to disrupt and destroy the Puerto Rican left. Its actions included planting stories in several newspapers in 1976 and 1977 (including the *New York Times*) about a terrorist network that stretched from Chicago to California, Colorado, New Mexico, and the Caribbean. FBI infiltrators encouraged factional conflicts among independence leaders.

Radio stations were threatened with the loss of their FCC licenses if they allowed pro-independence programming. FBI-generated defamatory articles were routinely printed in the mainstream media. High school teachers and public employees lived in fear of being fired for supporting Puerto Rican independence.

In 1973, Claridad, the organ of the Puerto Rican Socialist Party (PSP), was firebombed. Between 1973 and 1988, at least 170 beatings, shootings and bombings of pro-independence organizations and activists took place, not counting assaults and beatings at rallies and picket lines. In 1975 the anti-independence violence escalated with the bombing of a rally in the Puerto Rican city of Mayaguez, in which two restaurant workers were killed. No one was ever arrested for those crimes. In 1977 Teamster activist Juan Caballero disappeared. The FBI led investigators to the wrong body, after announcing that he had probably been killed by his own associates. When the ruse was discovered, the fingers of the cadaver were severed, sent to Washington for fingerprint investigation, and subsequently "lost."

In 1976 the son of Puerto Rican Socialist Party leader Juan Mari Bras was murdered. The FBI is suspected of having had a hand in the murder, or helping the perpetrators to escape. Many also believe the FBI was behind the firebombing of Mari Bras' home in 1978.

On July 25, 1978, two Puerto Rican youth, Carlos Soto and Arnaldo Dario, were enticed into bombing the TV tower on top of Puerto Rico's Cerro Maravilla Mountain by a provocateur, Alejandro Gonzalez. There, they were ambushed by the police, forced to kneel on the ground, tortured, and executed while begging for their lives. A witness courageously refused to remain quiet about the murders. A lengthy investigation revealed that the assassination had been planned in collaboration with the FBI.

On April 4, 1980, repressive forces of the United States arrested eleven Puerto Ricans in the suburb of Evanston, Illinois. They were immediately accused of membership in the Armed Forces of Puerto Rican National Liberation (FALN). The arrests took place at 4 PM and by 10 PM, the patriots had declared themselves "prisoners of war." From the international viewpoint, a prisoner of war is any combatant or reserve that, in any phase or circumstance of war, either by individual or collective surrender, or by being captured, falls into the enemy's hands. Regardless of your perspective on the legitimacy of a citizen of a U.S. territory to claim this role, it speaks to how the arrestees saw themselves.

Afterwards, a massive campaign was carried out to publicly denounce the psychological torture of arrestee Freddie Mendez. Mendez was subject to psychological torture and sophisticated "pressure" and brainwashing techniques until he became a mouthpiece of the federal authorities.

International Law is very specific in reference to prisoners of war. According to the Geneva Convention, combatants who have declared themselves prisoners of war must be recognized as such. Those arrested in Evanston were armed and accused of belonging to the Armed Forces of Puerto Rican National Liberation. The nature of the arrest and the U.S. government's own indictment serves to affirm that the eleven were combatants for Puerto Rican independence at the time of their arrests. According to the Geneva Treaty, ratified by the UN in 1949 and signed by the U.S., captured soldiers are prisoners of war. In a meeting on July 8, 1977, additional protocols were approved for the Geneva Convention, extending protections to combatants who struggle against colonialism and foreign intervention. Prisoner of war status was extended to all anti-colonial combatants.

In 1999 there was a Congressional movement to release some of the oldest Puerto Rican political prisoners in the U.S. with clemency. Release in all cases required a pledge of nonviolence and not associating with each other—even though many of them were family.

All 16 prisoners were supporters of the Armed National Liberation Front (FALN) and the Puerto Rican People's Army (EPB), also known as the "Macheteros," which carried out a series of bombings and other armed attacks on U.S. government offices and military installations in the 1970s and early 1980s. The Macheteros blew up 10 fighter jets in the 80's on the island of Puerto Rico that were going on bombing missions in Nicaragua.

No evidence was presented linking any of the defendants to specific acts of violence. All were convicted of conspiracy and sedition charges after brief trials in which they refused to participate, on the grounds that they did not recognize the authority of the U.S. government. Their prison sentences ranged from 35-105, with the longest for Luis Rosa, a 19-year-old just out of high school.

Even by the standards of the American justice system, these sentences were extreme. In comparison, the average sentence for murder between 1966 and 1985 was 22.7 years, and for rape 12.4 years. Only 12.8 percent of all federal prisoners have received sentences greater than 20 years. These sentences appear to be designed to intimidate militant political opposition to U.S. imperialism in Puerto Rico.

Even though most of these prisoners are from the Chicago area, they have been scattered throughout 11 federal facilities, as far away as Lompoc, California. While in prison they have helped teach literacy, Spanish, AIDS awareness, and other subjects to their fellow inmates, yet they have been subject to harsh treatment, including lengthy bouts of solitary confinement and physical assaults.

Over the past two decades, the viciousness of the sentences imposed on the prisoners and their principled conduct in prison have won them widespread sympathy in Puerto Rico and in Puerto Rican communities in the United States. This growing support culminated in a demonstration on August 29 in San Juan, Puerto Rico where 150,000 people rallied to demand their unconditional release.

The march, which included tens of thousands of trade union members as well as representatives of student and professional organizations, was a broad reflection of all political forces in Puerto Rico, with the exception of the right-wing statehood party, the PNP. In the following weeks the White House received petitions from 100,000 people for the unconditional release of the prisoners.

Armed struggle, military resistance, and whatever form of struggle that leads to the independence of nations that are colonized, invaded, and occupied by foreign military troops, is recognized as a right by the U.N. Puerto Rico, by virtue of being a colonial state, is supported by International Law.

The $7.1 million robbery of a Wells Fargo facility in 1983 by the ERB was used as an excuse for blanket sweeps of socialists and independence activists in 1985. In August of that year, the FBI invaded the homes and offices of scores of independentistas, destroyed much of their property, and confiscated their personal papers. Much of that material was later "lost." Thirty-seven independentistas were rounded up without being charged with a crime. Then-Attorney General Edwin Meese made no secret that the U.S. government considered support for Puerto Rican independence tantamount to terrorism.

On October 12, 1970, UN resolution 2621 approved by the General Assembly, declared colonialism an international crime. Said resolution reaffirmed the right of any intervened, colonized nation to utilize whatever form of struggle is necessary to obtain its independence.

Filiberto Ojeda Rios

Filiberto Ojeda Rios was born in Naguabo, Puerto Rico in 1933. He was an accomplished musician who played the trumpet and guitar. He was a founding member of the Puerto Rican Workers Party (PRTP) in 1976. Filiberto was also the leader of the "Ejercito Popular Boricua—Los Macheteros." Based in Puerto Rico, this clandestine group claimed responsibility

for many armed actions since 1978. Filiberto was on the FBI's most wanted list for years in connection with the September 12, 1983, armed robbery of $7.2 million from the Wells Fargo Depot in Hartford, Connecticut. The money from the robbery was reportedly used to assist the poor in Puerto Rico and to fund the Puerto Rican independence movement.

Ojeda-Rios was a controversial, eccentric, and charismatic figure. As the leader of the Ejercito Popular Boricua, or the Macheteros, he united many armed independence factions into a political movement. Ojeda-Rios was indicted by a grand jury in 1985 for participating in the 1983 Wells Fargo bank robbery and went underground in Puerto Rico in 1990, but continued to be a voice of the independence movement by giving radio interviews and writing newspaper articles.

The FBI found his residence from an informant who later called Rep. Jose Serrano's (D-NY) office and said he regretted ratting out Ojeda-Rios because he did not realize the FBI would kill him. The FBI conducted further raids on the homes of other suspected independence activists according to the office of Rep. Charles Rangel (D-NY).

The spartan house in which Filiberto Ojeda Ríos lived for six years and died did not hide the political leanings of its owner. A small banner with the red-and-green logo of the Boricua Popular Army (Los Macheteros) hung over the wooden balcony. A small Macheteros banner—generally regarded as a nod to the group's most lofty tenets of egalitarian existence—is not a notable or ominous sight in Puerto Rico. Still, the display was odd for a private man who had been incessantly searched for fifteen years after he freed himself of an electronic monitoring device and jumped bail in 1990.

His neighbors in the small hilly town of Hormigueros, eighty-five miles west of San Juan, only knew that the man who lived in that house was "Don Luis," an unassuming 70-something who enjoyed gardening. Silent and reserved, he used to wave at the neighbors from his farmhouse in the Plan Bonito (Beautiful Plan) sector whenever he saw them. There was no inkling of the leader who served as the emotional symbol of Puerto Rican national resistance for more than two decades and was regarded variously as icon, legend, hero, madman, or cowardly criminal once on the FBI's Most Wanted List for the infamous 1983 heist of the Wells Fargo truck. Earlier that year, the reward for information leading to his arrest was increased to $1 million, even though the Macheteros had been inactive for fifteen years.

But by midnight of September 23, Puerto Ricans just wanted to see Ojeda Ríos alive. It took twenty-four hours to finally learn, in a tense FBI press conference, that the bullet that entered his neck and exited through his back had killed him. This time he could not evade the exacting art of a sharpshooter, even wearing his faithful bulletproof vest.

The operation in which Ojeda Ríos was killed has singlehandedly turned the former fugitive from a Robin Hoodish patriot of reference into the consensual patriot of preference in Puerto Rico. Surrender was not an option for Ojeda Ríos. Armed with a federal arrest warrant, the agents contend that they found an armed fugitive. "He started the whole thing. He fired first and wounded an agent," said the FBI's Special Agent in charge, Luis Fraticelli. Ojeda Ríos's widow, Elma Beatriz Rosado Barbosa, who was briefly detained by agents at the house and then released, has countered that the FBI contingent entered the house firing. Apparently the bureau contemplated neither Ojeda Ríos's surrender nor his survival. The wounded agent was airlifted to a hospital. Ojeda was not. Special Agent Fraticelli said the FBI "feared explosives might be present in the house" and waited eighteen hours after they shot Ojeda Ríos for "fresh agents to arrive in a flight from Quantico to attempt a tactical entrance to the hideout." The autopsy performed on Ojeda Ríos's body revealed that his wound was not life threatening and that he could have survived if he had received proper medical attention. Instead, he slowly bled to death. Amnesty International suggested that the killing had the blueprint of an "extrajudicial execution."

Puerto Rican independence leaders termed the FBI intervention "a shameful spectacle, an unconscionable show of force" against the popular hero, but on this politically divided island even hard-line statehood advocates such as Resident Commissioner Luis Fortuno, along with pro-Commonwealth Governor Aníbal Acevedo Vilá, have aggressively chastised

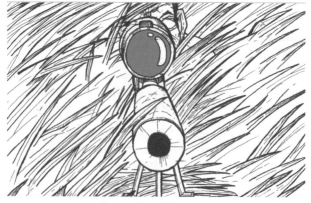

the FBI for its "highly irregular" procedures. The governor formally asked Washington for a thorough internal investigation and vowed to conduct his own. The three Puerto Rican members of Congress—Representatives Luis Gutierrez from Illinois, José Serrano, and Nydia Velazquez from New York—also pressed FBI Director Robert Mueller for an investigation. Mueller personally called Governor Acevedo Vilá to confirm that he had asked the Justice Department's Office of the Inspector General to conduct an "independent review" of the matter. An FBI spokesman added, however, "We have every reason to believe the agents acted properly."

Filiberto Ojeda Rios inspired generations of activists towards what they saw as a better, more humane world. Filiberto lived his life in the service of Puerto Rico, an example of "Valor y Sacrificio," which el Maestro Don Pedro Albizu Campos said the nation is built on.

More than 20 bullet casings were found at the crime scene, including some AR-15 shells. Ms. Rosado, who was also injured during the gun battle, said Filiberto's last words were "pa'lante siempre." He was 72 years old.

Appearing on *Democracy Now*, Jorge Farinacci, the spokesperson for the Puerto Rican Socialist Front said "The people of Puerto Rico, notwithstanding their political positions, understood clearly that this was a murder, that it was an arrogant and vengeful event planned by the FBI, and even though there are many differences within the Puerto

Rican community regarding our future, there's a lot of national pride. And Puerto Ricans don't like to be pushed, don't like to be harassed—our leaders could be murdered in cold blood without any kind of response. I think that the dignity of the Puerto Rican people was hurt very badly by this planned murder by the FBI."

Also appearing on *Democracy Now*, Juan-Manuel Garcia-Passalacqua, a Harvard-educated attorney and independent political analyst in Puerto Rico who hosts one of the islands most popular radio programs on Noti Uno, commented "I don't have any doubt whatsoever that the government of Puerto Rico contributed to that event by turning off the lights in the barrio where Filiberto Ojeda Rios lived. Over 200 houses were left without lights in the evening so that the sharpshooter with his laser and special rifle could kill Filiberto. There is no way that the lights could have been turned off in the barrio, without an expressed authorization of the electrical governmental company, and that order must have come, from the Fortaleza. And I am sure it will have to come out in the investigation by inspector general of the United States."

Edgardo Ojeda, son of Filiberto Ojeda Rios, testified in front of the UN Special Committee, describing what the family knows about the murder and later recounted how his father, while surrounded by hordes of FBI agents, demanded to meet with a reporter. Having this demand rejected, Ojeda Rios continued to resist the effort to assassinate him until the one bullet pierced his clavicle. Edgardo Ojeda proudly recounted how his father consistently and brazenly defied the agents who were obviously there to murder him, continuously yelling patriotic slogans from inside the house such as, "Asesinos Fuera de mi Patria," "Yanqui fuera de mi patria," "Que Viva Puerto Rico Libre," etc.

Independentistas organized massive protests in Puerto Rico, blocking the main highways in San Juan. Demonstrations were also organized in New York, New Jersey, Boston, and Chicago. A riot at the 23,000-student University of Puerto Rico forced administrators to decree an "academic recess" and allow professors, staff, and students to attend Filiberto's funeral. Filiberto's legacy will continue to live on in our history, our hearts, and within the struggle.

Jorge Farinacci also commented "El Grito de Lares is more or less like the Fourth of July. It's the day that we proclaimed our independence from Spain, although that revolution was crushed via the resistance. The desire for independence is always present in Puerto Rico for the last 150 years. And there's a commemoration of that date every year in Puerto Rico in the town of Lares. This time this year, thousands of thousands of Puerto Ricans, we gather in Lares to not only commemorate the Grito de Lares, but also to reaffirm our rights to self-determination, our right to independence, and a call for the end of the colonization that the United States has imposed on Puerto Rico."

"Since the last years, Filiberto Ojeda has constantly been present in Lares through video messages or audio messages that, when they come to the audience, everybody is silent to hear his message. His message this year was a message of unity, was a message of national reconciliation, and was a very positive message to the Puerto Rican people. And it's ironic that at the same time that that message was being made to be addressed to the public there, the FBI had 200 agents surrounding his house, preparing to murder him." To the chagrin of political opponents, two days after his death Ojeda Ríos's face had been fashioned into a cast by an artist, and the government announced that his house would be turned into a museum and the street leading to it would bear his name. The body was accorded all kinds of posthumous honors at the island's oldest cultural institution, the Ateneo Puertorriqueño, and, to the surprise of many, at the headquarters of the Puerto Rico Bar Association.

Hundreds of students overturned tables and chairs at the student center and entered food concessionaries. In a frenzy of unmitigated rage, everything that hinted at colonial domination was game. Hamburgers became projectiles as students scribbled with aerosol and ketchup on fast-food restaurant walls, striking against McDonald's and Burger King. Just as they did at an inpromptu gathering the day Ojeda Ríos died, thousands joined in a seven-hour motorcade on September 27, the day of his funeral, singing the Puerto Rican revolutionary hymn and shouting anti-U.S.

slogans. Scores of banners reflected popular anger: FEDERAL AGENTS=ASSASSINS; FBI: HERE YOU GO KILLING AGAIN; KILL FEDERAL PIGS. On the day that independence leaders had been chastised by Ojeda Ríos in his taped message for their lack of a unified front against the growing statehood forces, on the day that he vowed to keep on fighting "without opportunism, without hesitation," the FBI unwittingly rearranged the landscape of independence in Puerto Rico by granting instant martyrdom to the old fighter, uniting a partisan sea.

The death of Ojeda Ríos has meant more than the provisional rekindling of anti-U.S. rhetoric and flag burnings. While then Senator Hillary Rodham Clinton—perhaps concerned by the fact that she had publicly denounced the clemency granted to Puerto Rican political prisoners by President Clinton in 1999 and wanting to avoid controversy—canceled a planned visit to the island. Security was tightened in federal buildings.

Independence organizations, long beset by internal bickering and confused strategy, rapidly moved to present a united front. Even those who were not yet rallying for a common goal, rallied against a common adversary instead of against one another. "Few times have we hated so, and so united in our hate," said Julio Muriente, a university professor and co-leader of the Hostosiano Movement. Former political prisoner Lolita Lebron, who served twenty-five years in federal prison for opening fire at the U.S. House of Representatives in 1954, wounding five Congressmen, considers this the "most important historical moment" for independence supporters in Puerto Rico. "We must organize and think. We have to use our heads. Anything can happen now. I would vouch for no shots, no violent retaliation. This must be the start of a true ethical revolution."

Filiberto Ojeda Ríos once said that he had always felt "protected by the people." He was buried in his hometown of Naguabo, in a wooden casket adorned with a machete, and all the independence groups, the known and unknown acronyms, were there together, mourning. The Macheteros' response at the funeral was a terse statement, signed by the group's apparent new leader, Commader Guasabara. "[The

FBI] made a mistake. The trumpet of liberty still calls us to the struggle."

Instead of the death of the island's independence movement, death renewed the solidarity towards independence.

The Mutual Benefits of Empire

There is an often expressed assumption that Puerto Rico depends on U.S. assistance to avoid widespread poverty and starvation. Conversely, there are numerous examples of "over populated," independent, small island countries with few natural resources that are not starving or depending on other countries economic bail outs for support, including Singapore, Ireland, South Korea, Costa Rica, Luxembourg, and the Bahamas. They do not require massive aid and do not have the majority of their populations living in deprivation. Interdependentness among independent island nations has proven to be a sustainable economic model.

In the long run, independence would be doing a favor to the American economy. In every instance that someone in Congress or in the executive branch comments on Puerto Rican independence, they make it quite clear that there will be considerable economic aid. However, this is not an anomaly. The U.S. sends financial aid to nearly every country in this hemisphere, and would continue to have many commercial and manufacturing ties with Puerto Rico. The island would continue to receive substantial investments comparable to those presently coming in. It is fair and in the best interests of both the United States and Puerto Rico.

The potential for a successful Puerto Rico as an independent nation is often compared to other spanish speaking Carribean islands. Where is the logic that every Spanish-speaking country is the same as every other Spanish-speaking country? Are they somehow inferior to other nations? Each country is unique in and of itself, and depends to a great degree on its economic condition when and shortly after it becomes sovereign, on its trade agreements with other nations, its level of technology, its infrastructure, its level of education, and upon a multitude of other factors that do not include its language, its music, or its culture. To determine whether we have a shot at a successful economy, then compare it to Singapore, Ireland, South Korea, Taiwan, etc.

Puerto Rican leaders are inspired by the success of Fidel Castro in Cuba and believe they can be equally successful in Puerto Rico.

Independentist organizations assert that they are not controlled or dictated to by any outside groups. Nevertheless, the Independentistas' reliance on the Cuban delegation for support before the United Nations, the attendance of MPI and FUPI (Federacion Universitaria Pro-Independencia) delegates at meetings in Communist countries, and their anti-Vietnam War stands and pro-Hanoi statements, confirmed for the average Puerto Rican a link between independence and communism.

Empire may have some benefits but cancer rates in Vieques is not one of them, the sterilization of women is not one of them either, or the unemployment, or the damage to the enviornment, or the destablization of Puerto Rico's economy. Those aren't the benefits of empire. Nor are political prisoners or assassinations. The benefits of empire were put into place solely to benefit empire so let's not get it confused. The fact that Puerto Ricans have found a way to squeeze something out of the nothing that empire offers is more a testament to Puerto Rico than anything else. The assassination of Filiberto for Puerto Ricans was like the death of Che Guevara to Cubans. Filiberto was the FBI's number one fugitive (until 9/11) for a reason. And it's not because of the benefits that empire has brought.

The reason so many people are taking this issue of U.S. imperialism in Puerto Rico so lightly is because they don't see a resistance movement and that is principally because the U.S. government doesn't want them to see it. How does it look that the bastion of democracry and freedom in the world can lay claim to the oldest colony on the planet? The very same almighty U.S. can claim to bring democracry and freedom to Afghanistan and Iraq but can't see its way to freeing the oldest colony on the planet?

Repression, Fear, and Harrassment

In a move reminiscent of a U.S. Marine invasion of a foreign country, the FBI descended in droves on Puerto Rico on February 10, 2006. Without breathing a word of the invasion to either the colonial governor or the chief of police, heavily armed, militarized units of the FBI, including the Special Weapons and Tactics Unit from Miami, hit six different spots throughout the island. Their purpose, they claimed, was to execute search warrants on six independence activists they identified as suspected leaders of the clandestine independence organization, Ejercito Popular Boricua/ Macheteros, the same organization whose legendary leader, Filiberto Ojeda Ríos, the FBI assassinated five months earlier. Their true purpose was widely understood: with their show of force, to continue their long campaign to intimidate and criminalize those who support independence for Puerto Rico, particularly in this moment of the resurgence of the left throughout Latin America; and, of course, to detract from their own criminal conduct in taking Ojeda's life. "This is yet another move on the part of the FBI to control and warn those who advocate for the independence of Puerto Rico, exercising their constitutional rights. It appears they are sending a message of intimidation," said independentist activist and attorney Roxana Badillo, who added that they are sorely mistaken if they believe the movement will be intimidated.

Landing in military-style helicopters, accompanied by caravans of vehicles, sometimes with the license plates obscured, FBI agents swarmed private residences and businesses in Trujillo Alto and Río Piedras (in the San Juan metropolitan area), and Mayagüez, San Germán, Aguadilla, and Isabela (in the west of the island), terrorizing entire neighborhoods. The search warrants bore the names and addresses of veteran labor leaders, community leaders, known independentists, and even a Protestant minister respected for his work promoting small projects of self-empowerment for poor people. In Río Piedras, as Homeland Security helicopters hovered above and sharpshooters watched through their telescopes from neighboring buildings, FBI agents were ransacking the apartment of independentist Liliana Laboy. The Puerto Rican media arrived to cover the remarkable event. With the FBI's murder of Ojeda Ríos fresh on their minds, independence supporters quickly gathered at the closed gates of the condominium, shouting, "Asesinos!" Meanwhile, the FBI had banished Laboy from her apartment, and initially ignored requests from her attorneys to allow them access to their client, grabbing and threatening to arrest the attorneys if they didn't leave the premises.

In San Germán, agents assaulted the offices of the not-for-profit Ecumenical Committee for Community Economic Development [CEDECO, its Spanish acronym], where community activist and independentist William Mohler García was at work. They not only removed Mohler from his office, but they handcuffed him and left him to bake in the hot sun—this, after searching his home, pepper-spraying his dog, and subjecting his wife to much humiliation. Supporters gathered at the scene, shouting at the agents: "Get out of here, damned FBI," and "FBI, cowards, assassins, terrorists!" In Aguadilla, the FBI searched the home of another CEDECO director, Presbyterian minister and independentist José Morales. Also in Aguadilla, the FBI spent four hours searching the home of independentist and elementary school teacher VilmaVélez Roldán, while she was at school. Agents threw her two sons out of their home, handcuffed them, and left them outside with no shade.

Before leaving the scene in Río Piedras, the FBI, obviously unhappy with the presence of protesters and abundant numbers of media and the prospect of having to face further public exposure, aggressed against all those gathered, including attacking the media with pepper spray. Several journalists were treated by paramedics at the scene, and some went to nearby hospitals. As the caravan of some fourteen vehicles

Photo by Vanessa Serra

sped from the scene, the agents had their assault weapons pointed at the press and public. Adding insult to injury, the FBI emitted a press release stating, "It appears members of the media and the general public attempted to cross the established law enforcement perimeter, and the use of non-lethal force was utilized. This was done in order to protect members of the media, the public, and the law enforcement officers executing this lawful search warrant."

"The only domestic terrorist attack here is the U.S. government's attack on the people of Puerto Rico."
—New York State Assemblyman José Rivera

June 13, 2006—The special committee of the United Nations General Assembly that deals with decolonization issues today adopted a text calling for an expedited process in Puerto Rico to determine what kind of relationship the territory's population would prefer to have with the United States. The unanimously adopted resolution, sponsored by Cuba, calls for an investigation into the 23 September assassination of pro-independence leader Filiberto Ojeda Rios and violent acts against others. It also calls on the United States to respect fundamental human rights in Puerto Rico, pay for the clean-up and decontamination of areas of the island affected by United States military activities, and address the ensuing serious environmental and health consequences. As in previous years, the special committee's text called on the President of the United States to release Puerto Rican political prisoners serving prison sentences for more than 25 years for cases relating to the struggle for the independence of Puerto Rico and the demilitarization of Vieques Island, which had been used for combat exercises by the U.S. military.

Many petitioners speaking today and yesterday, including representatives of Puerto Rico's main political parties, supported the text, saying that the island's current relationship with the United States was deeply flawed and had stunted its socio-economic development and allowed the exploitation of its natural resources by American companies and the United States Navy.

Conclusion

One of the most common arguments against Puerto Rican independence is that the people don't want it; that it's not a popular movement. This is a product of many cultural factors and FBI and COINTELPRO scare tactics as well as a fear of losing U.S. resources that families have become dependent on.

The social price for individuals espousing Puerto Rican independence is high because Puerto Rican society demands a high degree of conformity. Close living is coupled with "an extreme dependency on the opinion of others," and a fear of being exposed to "what people will say." The belief in independence, particularly as it is associated with violence and communism, is not only an official liability but a personal one. Government repression and discrimination has been more effective because it is combined with social pressure.

The parallels and links to all eras of suppression of rebellion by our government and it's secret agencies are shocking in this present day example. I've been told repeatedly that COINTELPRO doesn't exist anymore; that politically motivated assassinations by the U.S. government are a thing of the past. Evil exists in the dark corners of the most powerful bodies in this country and it's not being reported when the incidents happen. If not for very miniscule scale independent media, articles, and the internet, I would not have learned that this atrociety occurred at all. This zine is a further step in that direction; to educate people that this occurs and put more information in one place; to show the striking similarities to the assassinations of other freedom fighters like Fred Hampton and Martin Luther King.

As you read this there are certainly more and more examples of this going on around the world. The Bush cabinents' wars in Afganistan and Iraq are horrible atrocities but often lead to us overlooking the covert ops going on under the radar by intelligence agencies around the clock.

Please think about the implications of the U.S. government assassinating a minor threat to their power from a territory that they occupy illegally. Fascism, anyone?

Further Reading/References:

Las Venas Abiertas de América Latin / *The Open Veins of Latin America* and *Memorias del Fuego* / *Memories of the Fire*

Democracy Now! Amy Goodman, Pacifica Radio

The Failure or Possibility of Puerto Rican Independence by Angelina Villafañe Faculty Mentor: Professor Patricia Hilden

Environmentalists Against War: FBI Murder of Puerto Rican Leader Condemned October 31, 2005

The Center for Constitutional Rights Statement on the Death of Filiberto Ojeda-Rios, Guerilla News Network: By Ari Paul

Counterpunch: The Contradiction is Between Yankees and Puerto Ricans FBI Home Invasions in Puerto Rico By Gervasio Morales Rodriguez

Monthly Review: FBI Commits Domestic Terrorism on Independence Movement in Puerto Rico by Jan Susler

Puerto Rico: A Colonial Experiment Carr, Raymond, Vintage Books, 1984

THE CIA MAKES SCIENCE FICTION UNEXCITING #5

The things you may not know about Iran/Contr

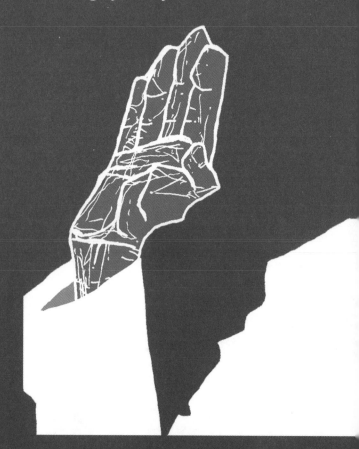

I became aware of Ollie North and the Iran-Contra scandal at the same time as most Americans who lived through the 80s. I have a clear memory of seeing Ronald Reagan give a press conference, downplaying the scandal as more and more information started to hit the media—proof that the President *had* sold arms to Iran in exchange for hostages. Some people still backed the President saying that his actions might have been illegal, but that they were justified considering the situation. Still, most people were dismayed. Shortly before the scandal broke, there was some talk about trying to amend the U.S. Constitution to allow Reagan to run for a third term in office. Luckily, the Iran-Contra scandal leaked and few talked about that crazy notion again.

Like many people across the world, I spent a good deal of the summer of 1987 stuck in front of the television, watching Lt. Colonel Oliver North give his speech about why he did what he did. I didn't realize it at the time, but later came to feel that I had been preached nothing more than propaganda. The Right Wing fear that the Nicaraguans were soon going to invade Texas was unfounded, and the means by which Reagan raised money for his pet causes was so unethical that little could justify what he authorized.

Because of Reagan and the staff of his administration, two incredibly bloody wars were prolonged for nearly the entire decade. In the Persian Gulf, the Iran-Iraq War saw a brutality that hadn't been witnessed since the First World War. Chemical Weapons were made available by Western powers that cost thousands of people their lives. Major cities were bombed, infrastructure damaged, and countless military and civilian deaths were caused by a war that neither side gained a thing from. By the time of the truce, over a million people had been killed, and the U.S. government had played a direct role in the gassing of Iranians while arming both sides.

In Nicaragua, Reagan's anti-communist rhetoric brought the U.S. that much closer to a full-scale military involvement. In Salman Rushdie's *The Jaguar Smile*, Rushdie recounts the fear of the Nicaraguan people of a U.S. invasion and what it would mean for the Nicaraguan people to see their country turned into another Vietnam. The CIA sponsored civil war cost over 30,000 Nicaraguans their lives and directly changed the course of their country, from which they're only now beginning to recover. In fact, I believe it was specifically because of Reagan's deeds in the Iran-Contra scandal, following a tragic path of U.S. meddling with Iran's destiny, that the U.S. was bogged down in our latest "Vietnam"—the war in Iraq. By playing games with the lives of millions of people and being held virtually unaccountable for it, the U.S. set the stage for two subsequent wars with Iraq. Still, people in government seem reluctant to learn a thing from the follies of history.

In 2008, when this text was originally published, President Bush was aggressively pushing for more military action against Iran. I don't think when President Eisenhower first authorized actions in Iran in the 1950s anyone would have dreamed where this path would lead to. This is a fundamental problem with U.S. foreign policy; the notion that it is in anyone's best interest to impede with a people's self-determination. Once that Pandora's Box is opened, you never know what will come out.

Sadly, much of the information about this case is still classified, mysterious history and you have to take what some people write with a grain of salt because they're all trained liars. There's a little conspiracy in here, but none that's not corroborated by other sources or backed up by credible witnesses. One guy in particular, Mansur Rafizedah, was the head of SAVAK (the Iranian CIA under the Shah). It's hard to tell if he's completely credible, but the info sounds right from the rest of the facts, and the *New York Times* used him as a credible source for a story on the October Surprise. He's at least as credible as any of his American counterparts, and didn't have anything really to gain or lose by lying—unlike the Americans.

The October Surprise material here is mostly taken from Gary Sick's book, written from first hand sources while he was in the White House and military under several presidents. Congress said it didn't happen, but others, including *The New York Times,* say it did. Please feel free to research this further. As always, sources and further reading are available at the end.

The Overthrow of Mohammad Mossadegh

Ever since oil was discovered in Iran in the first decade of the 20th century, British companies controlled the majority of Iranian oil fields. This oil was so crucial to British interests that Britain invaded Iran during the Second World War because Iran was thought to be friendly to Germany. The British quickly removed the Shah (the head of the Iranian monarchy), sent him into exile and replaced him with his son, Mohammad Reza Phahlavi. The new Shah knew firsthand that his best interest was to remain favorable with England, and keep British oil revenue in Iran secure.

After the war, Great Britain was in a far different position than it had been a few years earlier. The sun was setting on their empire, but the British refused to give up their possessions (otherwise known as countries, including Iran) without a fight. Under increasing pressure to return a higher percentage of oil royalties to the people of Iran, Britain refused. Negotiations went nowhere, and the situation deteriorated. There had also been strong calls for democratic reforms in Iran. The Shah had been reduced to a figurehead with little political support or real power. In March 1951, political turmoil raged in Iran as the pro-Western prime minister was assassinated. The following month, the Iranian parliament voted to nationalize its country's foreign-owned oil fields. Mohammed Mossadegh, a popular member of the Iranian parliament who helped spearhead the nationalization movement, was voted in to replace the slain prime minister.

The British-based Anglo-Iranian Oil Company (later British Petroleum, now simply BP), which received most of the oil profits from Iranian fields, was angry about the potential lost revenues and lobbied the British government to act to stop the nationalization. The World Court tried to intervene and work out a settlement between the two countries, but neither side could agree on a compromise. After the loss in the World Court, Great Britain, seeing that it wouldn't get its oil profits through legal channels, imposed a naval blockade of Iran in the hope that a strangulation of the Iranian economy would force Iran to reconsider nationalization.

Mossadegh was well aware of the stakes of nationalizing his country's oil industry. For the first time in its history,

Iran was taking in the majority of the profits generated by its natural resource. Mossadegh believed that if Iran didn't control its own resources, the country could not be independent and prosperous. However, by nationalizing the oil industry, he also knew that Iran faced foreign intervention in some form or another.

The government of Great Britain, led by Winston Churchill, wanted the nationalization problem solved as quickly as possible. In 1951, Churchill asked U.S. President Harry Truman for assistance in overthrowing Mossadegh, but Truman felt the current war in Korea was a higher priority. Britain, bogged down by post-WWII domestic issues and the further crumbling of its empire, was in no position to act on Iran by itself and decided to wait for a new U.S. President.

Ignoring the genuine desire of the Iranian people to control their own destiny, Britain had convinced itself that the Soviet Union, not Iran, was calling the shots in Tehran. Playing on the U.S. government's fears of an expanding communist influence throughout the world, Britain asked again for assistance in Iran as part of its war on international communism. In 1953, newly elected U.S. president Dwight Eisenhower agreed to Britain's request to covertly intervene in Iran on the side of the British. Operation Ajax was hatched out of this agreement.

Kermit Roosevelt Jr., grandson of Teddy Roosevelt, was chosen to head the CIA operation that entailed building a guerilla army, fomenting and manufacturing popular

discontent against Mossadegh, and readying a possible new regime to seize power when the time was right. Kermit Roosevelt was assisted by Norman Schwarzkopf Sr., father of Stormin' Norman, later of Desert Storm fame. Schwarzkopf Sr. helped convince the Shah that he should return to a position of full, supreme power when the time was right. Since the bulk of the Operation Ajax planning was to be done by these two Americans, they needed a safe place to run the show. Headquarters for the planning and execution of the operation were directly inside the U.S. Embassy in Tehran.

To aid in the coup, the British courted an Iranian military officer, Gen. Fazlollah Zahedi, who had little sympathy for the Communist Party or the USSR. The Shah, a man of little political power at this time, dismissed Prime Minister Mohammad Mossadegh and replaced him with Gen. Zahedi. Mossadegh had lost popularity due to the strain on the economy the embargo had, but would never have been deposed without the CIA's orchestration of a coup. Mossadegh was arrested on charges of treason, put on trial, and sentenced to death. The Shah later commuted his sentence to three years in solitary confinement and house arrest for the remainder of his life. Mohammad Mossadagh didn't die until 1967.

With Mossadegh incapacitated, in 1954 Gen. Zahedi worked out a deal with several foreign powers, most notably Great Britain and the U.S., to give Iran's oil fields back to the foreign companies. This arrangement lasted until the Iranian Revolution in 1979.

The Reign of the Shah and the Iranian Revolution
When the Shah took power and re-established the monarchy, he also moved to squelch dissent. His tool for suppressing opposition was an organization modeled after the CIA, and built with the assistance of the U.S. and Israel, called SAVAK. SAVAK was well-known for its brutality toward anyone who opposed the Shah in any way. From communists to clerics, few who criticized him publicly were spared torture at the hands of SAVAK.

Besides the communists, the Shah was concerned about religious opposition. At this time, Iran experienced a strong religious revival, in large part due to a backlash from the Shah's hostility towards religion. One of the leaders of this revival and opposition was a cleric named Ruhollah Khomeini, who spoke out several times against the Shah for his association with Americans and Israelis, whom many felt animosity towards because of their oppression of Muslims in Palestine. For this, Khomeini was arrested and imprisoned for 18 months.

When Khomeini's prison sentence was completed, he was exiled first to Turkey, then to Iraq, where he spent more than a decade. Fearful of the powerful Shiite cleric, Saddam Hussein eventually forced Khomeini to leave Iraq, a deed Khomeini never forgot or forgave. From Iraq, Khomeini lived briefly in France until events in Iran called him home.

Popular dissent against the Shah was widespread. People from most classes and of many political and religious persuasions supported the growing anti-Shah revolution, including the majority Shiite population that looked to Khomeini for leadership, as they did before his exile. Khomeini's message of an Islamic revolution was spread through cassette recordings of his speeches, which were sold in markets throughout Iran. Simultaneously, the Shah was getting more antagonistic towards Iran's religious population.

According to Mansur Rafizadeh, former chief of SAVAK, the Shah hosted hundreds of art and music festivals that were held throughout the year, mostly with heavily anti-religious themes. These festivals were perceived to be blasphemous by religious Iranians, and such blasphemy—along with growing frustration over the economy and official repression of secular and religious opposition—caused the Shah's image to worsen. In 1979, the Shah left Iran, supposedly temporarily. He never returned.

On February 1, 1979, Khomeini returned to Iran to lead the revolution and, eventually, the revolutionary government. Meanwhile, the Shah, "on the run," suffered from rapidly deteriorating health. He desperately needed medical treatment for Lymphoma. After bouncing around from country to country, the Shah landed in the U.S. briefly for medical treatment reluctantly authorized by President Jimmy Carter. The Shah's stay was brief, but it seriously damaged Carter's image in Iran. The Iranian people felt that the U.S. was once again involving itself in their affairs. The revolutionary government of Iran demanded the return of the Shah so that he could stand trial back in his home country, but Carter refused to hand him over.

In part as a response to Carter's giving temporary asylum for the Shah, but also as a tactical move, student revolutionaries—the backbone of the Iranian revolution—planned a takeover of the U.S. Embassy in Tehran. It's important to remember that the U.S. Embassy had been the headquarters for the CIA-led coup against their democratic government in 1953. This new generation of Iranians that rallied around the memory of the Mossadegh coup was determined that this would not happen again.

Besides being a strategic target that could be used to overturn a revolution and possibly help restore the Shah to power, the U.S. Embassy was also an obvious symbolic target. Eleven years prior, the U.S. Embassy in Saigon had been briefly overrun by the Viet Cong. While not a military victory, the Saigon embassy attack was viewed with great symbolism and was a turning point in the U.S. war against the Vietnamese people. This incident was fresh in the minds of many of the Iranian students who occupied the U.S. Embassy in Tehran on Nov. 4, 1979.

One of the banners they used in the embassy takeover read, "Uncle Sam: Vietnam hurt you. Iran will bury you." Contrary to myth surrounding the Tehran embassy takeover, many of the students were not religious fanatics but secular leftists. In fact, much of the movement to dispose of the Shah was led by coalitions of religious and secular radicals who desperately wanted an end to religious and political repression. The majority of the Iranian population—not just the radicals—was also in opposition to the Shah's rule.

The Iranian Revolution was bound to happen sooner or later. By taking over the U.S. Embassy, the Iranian students sought to ensure that the U.S. could not overthrow the popular movement of 1979 as easily as it had executed the CIA-backed coup of 1953. When the U.S. Embassy was occupied by revolutionary Iranian students, initially all 66 Americans there were held as hostages. Then, in an act of solidarity with oppressed people, the Iranians freed most of the African-American and female hostages. Later, one more hostage was released for medical reasons. The remaining 52 hostages would be held for 444 days.

"The October Surprise"

Immediately after the U.S. Embassy was stormed by Iranian students, President Carter's popularity surged as Americans rallied behind their president. However, as the hostage crisis dragged on, it began to affect Carter's image. Carter became more desperate to end the crisis. He approved a rescue mission that ended in dismal failure when two helicopters filled with U.S. Army Special Forces teams crashed in the desert and killed everyone aboard. Carter took responsibility for the incident, which left him with an aura of helplessness and weakness.

1980 was an election year in the U.S., a fact of which the Iranians were well aware. The U.S. was beginning to go through a recession that was due in part to an increase in oil prices, driven by the instability in Iran. Carter's approval ratings in the U.S. seemed to plummet with each passing day. One of the primary reasons that the Iranians continued to hold the U.S. hostages was specifically because the hostage crisis was embarrassing the U.S. President. Another reason for the length of the hostage crisis, it has been alleged, was that the Committee to Elect Ronald Reagan prolonged the crisis through secret deals with the Iranians—aimed at further embarrassing Carter before Election Day, 1980.

The Reagan-Bush Campaign was helped immensely by the ongoing hostage crisis. The CIA in particular thought a Reagan-Bush presidency would be in their best interest. After all, Reagan's campaign manager, William Casey, was ex-military intelligence and would-be Vice-president George Bush had led the CIA a few years earlier. The Carter Administration had come into office in the years following former President Richard Nixon's abuses with a pledge to clean up the agency. Shortly after becoming president, Carter cut the number of active CIA agents by two-thirds. Many in intelligence felt burned by Carter and were eager to see him ousted. They saw their opportunity in Iran.

The Republican Party had many connections in the international intelligence field, and some thought that this would be a good time to use those connections. The mission, spearheaded by William Casey, sought to make certain that Carter would not gain politically from a release of the hostages before the 1980 election: an *October Surprise*, as Casey's team called it. Even though none of the Reagan staff were actually in government at the time, they were able to use complex networks of former and current intelligence officers to help gain inside information on Carter's efforts to free the hostages. Closer to the election, the Reagan-Bush campaign held secret meetings in Europe with Iranian emissaries and spelled out their position: If the Iranians waited until after the election to free the hostages, Reagan would make it worth their while. Meanwhile, tensions between Iraq and Iran were simmering.

Iraqi President Saddam Hussein was concerned that Shiite Muslim Iran was trying to spread its Islamic revolution to the majority Shiite population of Iraq. Further escalating tensions, an Iranian had attempted to assassinate Tariq Aziz, a close friend of Hussein's and deputy prime minister of Iraq. Iraq-Iran border skirmishes were on the rise. Feeling that Iran was in a weak position militarily, Hussein decided to use the somewhat chaotic situation in Iran to his advantage. The revolutionary Iranian government was going through its own purges of "counter-revolutionaries" (leftists, mostly) in its assertion of the Ayatollah's theocracy. Many of the top officers in Iran's military who hadn't fled were either in prison or dead; leaving Iran in a poor position to defend itself from an invasion. Seeing an opportunity to stop the spread of the Islamic Revolution and protect his regime, Hussein launched a pre-emptive strike into Iran. He felt the war would be over in a matter of months. It lasted eight years.

Iran had plenty of military aircraft and munitions, mostly purchased from the U.S. while the Shah was in power. Their main problems were a shortage of trained military officers and a lack of spare parts. After Iran was attacked, officials in the new Iranian government lobbied to free most of the military officers and use them to defend Iran against Iraq. This helped to solve half of Iran's military problems. However,

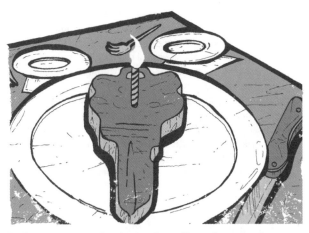

finding spare parts for the Iranian military fleet wasn't so easy to resolve. It was easy to get high-tech military equipment on the black market, but the Iranians found it nearly impossible to get routine items such as ball bearings and tires through those same channels. Conveniently, William Casey and the CIA entered the picture.

William Casey was a military intelligence officer during the Second World War and a good friend of Ronald Reagan, who asked Casey to manage his 1980 campaign and eventually head the CIA. It has long been alleged that Casey and his CIA connections spent a great deal of time behind the scenes making secret deals with Iran to provide the spare parts it needed in the war against Iraq. To do this, the Reagan-Bush team exploited Iranian animosity toward the Carter Administration. The case was made that there was little hope that arms could be shipped to the Iranians under a Carter presidency because of hard feelings over the hostages. Under a Republican regime, however, such shipments could and would be made through third-party countries. These third parties were necessary since Carter had imposed an arms embargo on Iran.

Essential to the Reagan-Bush team's plan was an agreement that Iran would hold the hostages until the election. The Reagan-Bush campaign knew that if Carter were to pull off an *October Surprise*—a release of the U.S. hostages at the last minute—it would be nearly impossible to defeat Carter. This was the greatest threat to Reagan and his followers' ambitions. It was crucial to ensure that the hostages were not harmed, but also not released, until November 1980.

The Reagan-Bush campaign allegedly worked covertly to orchestrate a favorable resolution of the hostage crisis. Carter desperately tried to free the hostages, but ultimately failed in his efforts. When the 1980 election took place, the hostage crisis became the main issue and eventually cost Carter his presidency.

To further humiliate the president who had given temporary safe-haven to the Shah and refused to send him back to Iran for trial, the Iranians held the hostages for the remaining days of Carter's presidency even after the election resulted in a Reagan-Bush win. On January 19th, President Carter announced, "an agreement with Iran will result, I believe, in the freedom of our American hostages." The response from the Reagan camp, the day before Reagan was to be inaugurated: "This administration will not negotiate with barbarians or terrorists."

Moments after Ronald Wilson Reagan was sworn in as the 40th president of the U.S., the revolutionary government of Iran gave the official announcement that the 52 remaining U.S. hostages would be freed. The former hostages immediately boarded a jet in Tehran bound for the U.S. Controversy still lingers over this series of events.

The Reagan Administration has always denied any collusion with the Ayatollah before Reagan took office. However, former Iranian president Abolhassan Beni-Sadr and Reagan campaign manager Barbara Honegger both claimed that these secret negotiations did occur, and continue to hold these claims. While evidence about the *October Surprise* plot is inconclusive, future events continued to make the scenario much more plausible. It foreshadows the trail of deception that came to be known as the Iran-Contra Scandal.

Revolution in Nicaragua

The end of the Seventies saw, not only a revolution in Iran, but another halfway around the world, in Nicaragua. In 1979, West

Point graduate and longtime Nicaraguan dictator Anastasio Somoza was overthrown in a popular revolution that, like the Iranian Revolution, brought a coalition government into power. This coalition was called the Sandinistas, named after the legendary Nicaraguan rebel Augusto Sandino.

The Sandinistas were made up of factions from all spectrums of the political arena, from the Catholic Church to the Communist Party of Nicaragua. Soon after the overthrow of Somoza, splits emerged in the new Sandinista government that pushed the coalition decidedly to the left, with Daniel Ortega emerging as the president. Others, in frustration, left and joined the opposition.

Initially, the U.S. government under President Carter was tacitly supportive of the new government in Managua. However, when Reagan came into office and the Sandinistas grew closer to the communist Soviet Union and Cuba, the U.S.-Nicaraguan relationship quickly cooled. President Reagan made overturning the Sandinista revolution a top priority. To do this, the U.S. needed to build on the scattered opposition to the popular Sandinistas. This was done mainly by the CIA, who recruited former officers and troops from Somoza's National Guard, to be led by Adolfo Calero. Taking their name from the Spanish word for "against", this army would be known as the Contras.

Adolfo Calero was the perfect pick to lead this army and be the Contras' main spokesperson. Calero gave the Contras credibility inside and outside Nicaragua. Besides being an outspoken part of the middle-class opposition to Somoza, Calero was the manager of Coca-Cola's Managua branch and a former CIA informant. At Reagan's request, the U.S. Congress hastily appropriated funds to give to the Contras. However, a series of high-profile cases of human rights abuses quickly eroded American support for this CIA-funded Contra army. Many were deeply wary of what "another Vietnam" could do to the U.S.

In this political atmosphere, the first Boland Act was made into law by Congress. The law prohibited the funding of the Contras in hopes that the U.S. would not be dragged into the Nicaraguan civil war. Whatever support remained for funding the Nicaraguan opposition slipped further when it was discovered that the CIA had played a key role in what was essentially an act of war against the people of Nicaragua: the mining of Managua Harbor.

The CIA's mining of Managua Harbor was condemned in the World Court as an act of aggression against the people of Nicaragua by the government of the U.S. The U.S. dismissed the World Court's decision, but this covert action was one of the straws that broke the congressional back concerning the possibility of future funding for the Contras. On Dec. 12, 1984, the second Boland Amendment was signed into law. This law essentially cut off funds to the Contras at least until late 1985. The Boland Amendment also made it illegal for people in the U.S. government to circumvent this law by seeking out funding for the Contras through third countries.

Reagan, often defiant of popular will, would not let these amendments stop funding for the Contra War against the Sandinistas. The fact that it was now illegal to fund the Contras was not enough to halt Reagan and his band of anti-communist zealots. Reagan told his national security advisor to find a way to keep the "body and soul" of the Contras together until legal funding could be found. The person put in charge of this mission was a right-wing ideologue and Vietnam vet, Marine Lt. Col. Oliver North. Because it was illegal for the U.S. to officially or secretly fund the Contras, Reagan turned to third countries and private sources to find money to continue the war in Nicaragua despite the Boland Amendment.

Between Reagan, the national security advisor, and National Security Council staff, 34 million dollars was raised from three countries. An additional 2.7 million dollars came from private contributors (often in exchange for private photo shoots with the president). Simultaneously, the Administration was publicly telling Congress (and the American people) that they were not soliciting funds from either private sources or other countries because, as they publicly acknowledged, the Boland Amendment forbid such actions on behalf of the Contras. Saudi Arabia was among the first countries to answer the call to support the Contras.

One million dollars a month was sent directly from Saudi Arabia to a bank account operated by Adolfo Calero himself. After it was discovered that improprieties existed, Lt. Col. North took over this bank account. Soon, all money being sent to help aid the Contras went directly into a Swiss bank account established by retired Air Force Gen. Richard Secord, another Vietnam veteran with experience in covert operations. Using the funds raised for support of the Contras (and eventually funds generated by the sale of weapons to Iran), Secord and his associate, an Iranian named Albert Hakim, started a covert private organization known as *The Enterprise*.

According to the Congressional report, *The Enterprise*, led by North, had "its own airplanes, pilots, airfield, operatives, and secret Swiss bank accounts." For almost a year and a half, *The Enterprise* worked as the secret arm of the National Security Council and ran off private and unaccountable funds completely against the law. Their main priority was not the legality of their mission, but prolonging the Contra War by any means necessary...and not getting caught.

The Weapons Sales Begin

Under the Shah, Mansure Rafizadeh was chief of Iran's clandestine service, SAVAK. He testified that in September 1981, eight months after the American hostages were freed in Tehran, William J. Casey, the director of the CIA, met with President Reagan and proposed selling arms to Iran. The rationale was that sending arms to Iran would facilitate contact between the Reagan campaign and the Islamic government, as well as enhance Casey's ability to gain intelligence by making direct contacts in the Iranian military.

The U.S. was not the only country looking to restore its previous client status with Iran. Just as the CIA had built many strong relationships within the Shah's despotic regime, so had Israel and Mossad (Israel's version of the CIA). SAVAK, the feared henchmen of the Shah, was modeled after the CIA but trained by Israel. Documents seized during the U.S. embassy takeover (and sold on the streets of Tehran) proved beyond a shadow of a doubt that both the U.S. and Israel had been involved in the internal affairs of Iran for years. In response, following the Iranian Revolution, chants of "Death to America" and "Death to Israel" were often heard.

In September 1981, despite a U.S. embargo on the sale of weapons to the Iranian government, Reagan signed an executive order to allow U.S. arms, sold through Israel, to be traded in kind from Israel's arsenal and delivered to Iran. While this certainly violated the intention of the embargo, it also violated the letter of the law. However, the Reagan Administration was not concerned with the implications of arming the same people that it called a "terrorist state." Nor did the Administration seem to consider how giving weapons to warring parties could prolong a bloody war or even endanger the lives of Americans later.

The concerns centered on achieving the Administration's shortsighted goals. So the official arms deals with Iran began. While one justification for the Reagan Administration illegally selling arms to Iran was the potential for closer relations between the U.S. and Khomeini's revolutionary government, the arms deals failed to give the Reagan Administration any real inroads into the Iranian government. Khomeini felt that, by trading arms with the Americans, he was making a deal with the "Great Satan" himself. Iran was in an awkward position. The Iran-Iraq War was far from over, and the Iranian military had begun to run out of spare parts. The Reagan regime believed that, by providing the spare parts that Iran desperately needed to win its war against Iraq, the Administration had Khomeini in its clutches.

While officially unfriendly to the new Iranian government, the Reagan Administration was also home to people fearful of an Iraqi victory because Iraq was thought to be in the "communist camp." Iraq was not an official satellite state of the USSR, but it was certainly a client state. Still, this CIA fear of Iraq's leftist leanings was unfounded considering Saddam Hussein's recent persecution of the Iraqi Communist Party. Hussein was a politician who used people, as needed, to remain in power and achieve his goals—a particular goal at this moment being victory against Iran and the Soviet Union was helping him to achieve this.

Hussein's relations with the USSR grew more intimate, not out of ideology, but out of need: the USSR armed the Iraqi military. Thus, many argued that the U.S. should support Iraq to lessen the possibility of Russia and Iraq getting closer. At the same time, others in the Reagan Administration felt it was more in America's interest to support the Iranians, despite the official rhetoric from the Iranian and American governments. The rationale behind the U.S. secretly supporting the Ayatollah Khomeini lay partly in a Cold War mentality. During the Carter Administration, some foreign policy "experts" theorized that radical Islam was the best weapon in the fight against the spread of "godless communism" in the Middle East. As Americans discovered on Sept. 11, 2001, however, there are repercussions to this train of thought. But during the Carter and Reagan administrations, support was strong for the arming of Islamic extremists in Iran. The movement to overthrow the Shah of Iran had been comprised of different factions, from deeply religious Muslims to extremely secular communists and anarchists. Once the Shah was gone, the fundamentalists were able to wrestle power from the leftists and establish the Islamic Republic. Soon after, the communists were forced to go underground again.

In one of many dubious moves on the part of CIA chief William Casey, the CIA was tasked with establishing contact with—and funding—not only the Iranian government, but also its opposition. The Reagan Administration and the CIA consistently acted in the most deceptive fashion. They gained trust with some while betraying others, once it became politically expedient to do so.

In 1982, a high-ranking KGB official, who had previously worked the Soviet's Iranian desk, defected to the West. After thorough interrogations, the KGB official gave American and British governments the Soviet intelligence on Iran, including contacts within the Iranian Tudeh (Communist) Party. The British held this information in confidence, but the Americans felt they could use it to their benefit. Two years after gaining the list of communist contacts in Iran, the CIA handed the list over to Khomeini as a sign of "goodwill." According to Rafizadeh, the former SAVAK chief, Khomeini had them all immediately arrested. Hundreds were executed and hundreds more languished for years in prison.

Second Round of Hostages

A pivotal moment in the Iran-Contra Affair took place in 1982 when David Dodge, the president of the American University of Beirut, was abducted in Lebanon. Dodge was the first of many Americans taken hostage, beginning what would become the second American hostage crisis. His Lebanese kidnappers were said to have close ties with Iran, and the U.S. believed Iran might be calling the shots. Despite the hostage-taking, money flowed to Iran from the U.S. in a futile effort to build closer ties to the Islamic Republic. While conflicted over the money, Iran was in no position to refuse it as much of the Middle East was in turmoil.

Besides the ongoing war between Iran and Iraq, Lebanon was in the middle of a very bloody civil war. Other countries joined in the fighting, most notably Israel and Syria. After Israeli armed troops were implicated in the massacre in the Sabra and Shatilla Palestinian refugee camps, the U.S. joined in U.N. peacekeeping forces in Beirut. On October 23, 1983, that U.S. force came under attack when the Marine barracks in Beirut were bombed. More than 200 Marines and sailors were killed. The bombing was blamed on the Iranian-backed Lebanese Shiite militia, Hezbollah.

According to Rafizedah, just prior to the attack, a great deal of American money was sent from Khomeini to Hezbollah for the sole intention of attacking American interests. The Marine barracks may have been one of those interests. (For a comprehensive look at the war in Lebanon, read Robert Fisk's *Pity the Nation*).

On March 16, 1984, Beirut's CIA station chief, William Buckley, was kidnapped. Buckley was viewed as a security risk for the CIA, as he was a known womanizer and had been exposed as a CIA operative a few years prior. Still, Buckley was sent to head the volatile Beirut desk. His subsequent kidnapping sent deep shock waves into the intelligence community because, for reasons unknown, they felt somewhat invincible to the violence that they often exacted on others throughout the world.

Buckley was held for more than a year. He was tortured and eventually died of medical neglect. Soon, more Americans would be taken hostage in Lebanon. In June 1985, hijackers took control of a TWA passenger plane, forcing it to land in Beirut. The hijackers, Lebanese Shiites, killed a U.S Navy diver and threw his body onto the tarmac. The remaining passengers were held for 16 days. A few days into this crisis, Reagan stated in a televised national press conference, "Let me further make it plain to the assassins in Beirut and their accomplices, wherever they may be, that America will never make concessions to terrorists—to do so would only invite more terrorism—nor will we ask nor pressure any other government to do so. Once we head down that path, there would be no end to it, no end to the suffering of innocent people, no end to the bloody ransom all civilized nations must pay."

At the end of the hijack crisis, Reagan showed even more bravado by saying, "Boy, after seeing *Rambo* last night, I know what to do the next time this happens."

Less than a month later, Reagan—in a move uncharacteristic of Rambo—gave his National Security Advisor, Robert McFarlane, a green light to pursue secret arms deals with the Iranian government through arms dealer Manucher Ghorbanifar. Ghorbanifar, an Iranian expatriate thought to be a double agent for Mossad, had a dubious record as a fabricator of intelligence, even within the CIA, which had plenty of experience in fabricating intelligence. This background didn't stop North and McFarlane from continuing to use "Ghorba" as a middleman even, as they both admitted later, they knew him to be a liar. In fact, deception seemed to have become the game in this affair, and everyone—from the bottom to the top—appeared to play the game well. The Reagan Administration claimed that it engaged in deception only out of concern for the fate of the U.S. hostages in Lebanon. The Administration said it was desperate to try anything to gain their release. However, this line of reasoning omits from the historical record the fact that Reagan Administration had planned to sell arms to the Iranians since well before the first hostages were taken under Reagan's watch.

In the summer of 1985, when the National Security Council was already involved in ongoing covert actions with Secord and *The Enterprise*, the government of Israel proposed that missiles be sold to Iran in exchange for the release of the hostages (now numbering seven). According to the Congressional report, the "Secretaries of State and Defense repeatedly opposed such sales to a government designated by the U.S. as a supporter of international terrorism."

The secretaries' main arguments were that this proposed deal would violate the U.S. public policy of not making concessions to terrorists and that it was illegal on two counts: the Arms Export Control Act and an arms embargo against Iran that had been in place since the '79 embassy takeover. Still, these objections were not strong enough to halt Reagan and the National Security Council. Reagan authorized Israel to proceed with the sales.

Between August and September of 1985, Israel sent Iran—supposedly an ideological enemy of the Israeli state as well—504 TOW anti-tank missiles. Iran had told the Israelis and Americans that all the hostages would be released after the weapons were transferred. Instead, only one was released. Despite this setback, Reagan insisted that Israel continue to send weapons to Iran.

In November 1985, Reagan authorized 80 HAWK anti-aircraft missiles to be sent from Israel, plus 40 more HAWK missiles directly from the U.S. In the end, only 18 missiles were sent, but no more hostages were released.

To help defray the costs of the transfer, Israel had advanced *The Enterprise* (North, Secord, and Hakim's secret government) $1 million. Since only 18 missiles were actually sent, this left *The Enterprise* with $800,000. North ordered that this money be used for his other project: the Contras.

Diversion of Funds to the Contras

On December 6, 1985, North told Israeli defense officials that his plans were now to send the profits on all future arms sales with Iran directly to the Contras in Nicaragua. The following day, the president and his top national security advisors had a meeting to discuss the arms sales. According to the Congressional report, the Secretaries of State and Defense objected to the deal on the grounds that the arms sales were illegal. Robert McFarlane agreed and said that the arms sales between Iran and Israel should be halted. Opposing this viewpoint were Admiral Poindexter (the newly appointed

National Security Advisor) and William Casey of the CIA, who both argued that, despite the law, the arms sales should continue.

The President sided with Poindexter and the CIA chief, and the rest fell in line. One month later, Reagan authorized another shipment of arms to Iran with the hope that more hostages would be released. The CIA's General Council again pointed out that this was in violation of the Arms Export Control Act. To circumvent this law, Reagan's Attorney General Ed Meese instead advised Reagan to have the weapons sent to Iran directly from the U.S., via *The Enterprise*. By this time, North had concluded that selling arms to Iran might never result in the release of any hostages. However, the incredible profit from the arms sales could be used to fund the Contras, as well as other covert operations in which *The Enterprise* was involved. While both North and Poindexter later claimed ignorance of where the money actually went, it is believed that the Contras received little of these profits.

In February 1986, the U.S., via *The Enterprise*, sold 1,000 TOW missiles to Iran. Again, no hostages were released, but North and Company made a killing (in the economic as well as literal sense). According to North in his testimony to Congress, CIA director William Casey approved of the diversion of funds and saw this as part of the bigger plan to fund all of Reagan's secret missions, with a nearly complete lack of accountability. Even though his unethical and illegal scheme had sent hundreds of thousands of dollars and thousands of weapons to warring countries, with costs unknown in Iraqi and Iranian lives with only one freed hostage to show for it, President Reagan decided to try it again. This time, the U.S. would send Iran parts for the HAWK missiles but on the condition that all the U.S. hostages held in Lebanon be released first. In one of the strangest episodes in U.S. "intelligence" history, Robert McFarlane, who had recently "retired" as the National Security Advisor, and a small contingent traveled secretly to Iran to personally deliver the HAWK missile parts.

McFarlane said later that he felt that the mission he was undertaking was similar to that of Henry Kissinger's secret meetings with Chou En-Lai that helped open relations between the U.S. and China. The result was less successful.

McFarlane and crew traveled to Tehran via Israel under fake Irish passports, without even attempting to get documents from Iran guaranteeing their safe conduct. McFarlane was supposed to attend a meeting with Iranian Speaker Rafsanjani to discuss the arms transfer in exchange for the release of all U.S. hostages (who, again, weren't actually being *held* by the Iranian government in Iran, but by Hezbollah in Lebanon. Hezbollah was supported by and sympathetic to Iran, but not an official arm of the Iranian government and, thus, Iran could probably not promise a release of these American hostages, even if it wanted to). The meeting was setup by Manucher Ghorbanifar, supposedly the very person responsible for the kidnapping of CIA agent William Buckley.

The trip started off bad and never got better. First, the timing was poorly planned as they traveled during the Islamic holiday of Ramadan. Many of the very people that they wanted to meet with had religious obligations and most were fasting during their negotiations. Then, to show the Iranians that they were serious, the team traveled with special gifts for the Ayatollah himself—a chocolate cake, a vaguely anti-Jewish verse from the Qur'an, two Colt pistols, and a bible inscribed by Ronald Reagan himself.

The chocolate cake had a key-shaped medallion on it that was a replica of the ones that the Iranian army wore into battle. Supposedly, this was North's idea. Reagan also sent a verbal message relayed by the delegation that said that he swore on the autographed Bible that the U.S. understood how genuine the Islamic revolution was, that he eagerly sought out the Iranian people's friendship, and, most importantly, that he should be trusted.

In *Witness*, Mansur Rafizadeh described the reaction: "The Iranian officials who received this odd assortment of gifts sent on behalf of the president of the U.S. were taken aback by what they could only interpret as his insensitivity or stupidity." The autographed Bible was considered the most offensive by the Muslims, who viewed the defacing of a holy book (be it the Old Testament, the New Testament, or the Torah, etc) as sacrilegious. Persian literature had always portrayed Jesus as the prophet who advocated "the turning of the other cheek" and nonviolence, so they were baffled by the contradiction of a Christian president sending both a Bible and Colt pistols. But they felt the most ludicrous aspect of these gifts was the selection of verses from the Koran that admonished the Jews for calling themselves chosen to the exclusion of other men.

How could the White House send this quotation as a message to Khomeini and simultaneously honor U.S. friendship with Israel? The end result of the cadre's "gift blessing" was that the Iranian officials now believed that President Reagan was either a fool or trying to fool them." This mission, of course, ended in failure for McFarlane, North, and the rest of the CIA/*Enterprise* crew that sponsored and supported it. No agreements were made and no hostages were released.

Over the summer of 1986, there would be even more setbacks for the Administration and *The Enterprise*. In the Miami Herald, an article titled *Despite Ban, U.S. Helping Contras*, began to expose the Reagan Administration's disregard for the congressional prohibition. Another story featured on a CBS news magazine revealed the private aid network that had been set up illegally to fund the Contras.

Because of the attention given to these articles, Congress began to look into the allegations against Colonel North and his staff. The Washington Post picked up on the story and ran an article on the Contra funding that caused North to offer his resignation to Admiral Poindexter. It was not accepted.

One small victory for The Enterprise came on July 26 when Reverend Lawrence Jenco, a U.S. hostage seized in Lebanon a year prior, was freed. A few days later, Vice President Bush was briefed, by the Israelis, on weapons sales to Iran, while Colonel North was forced to testify in front of Congress about the alleged Contra funding stories. In his testimony, North lied and told them that no aid was raised for the Contras by his office or provided by the CIA. If North thought their mission was succeeding, events in Lebanon, Nicaragua, and Washington would bring him back to reality.

In Lebanon, a pattern was occurring. As one hostage was released, another was kidnapped to take their place. Between September 6 and October 21, three American citizens were kidnapped in Lebanon. Then, on the other side of the planet, the mission to re-supply the Contras began to unravel.

On October 5, a plane owned by *The Enterprise* was shot down over Nicaragua by the Sandinistas. "Tragically," two of the three CIA agents aboard died. The third, a man named Eugene Hasenfus, disobeyed the CIA's orders not to wear a parachute and was the only survivor of the crash. He was captured the next day. For his actions, Hasenfus was tried and sentenced by the Nicaraguan government to 25 years in prison, but was released by Nicaraguan President and Sandinista leader Daniel Ortega less than two months later at the request of U.S. Senator Chris Dodd. But the damage was done. Hasenfus' capture and trial publicly exposed and gave proof to the allegations that the Reagan Administration was illegally aiding the Contras.

Meanwhile in Lebanon, yet another American was taken hostage in Lebanon. In response, on October 28 the U.S. sent 500 TOW missiles to Iran. The following day, General Secord and Colonel North were informed by Iranian delegates that students in Tehran were distributing a pamphlet that disclosed the McFarlane "Chocolate Cake" meeting. A final victory for *The Enterprise* came a few days later when American hostage David Jacobson, held for over a year, was released.

Then, on November 3, 1986, the plot completely unfolded. Lebanese magazine, *Al-Shiraa* ran a story that disclosed in detail the Chocolate Cake visit by McFarlane to Tehran. More importantly, the article detailed how the U.S. had been sending arms to Iran in exchange for hostages held in Lebanon for years. The cat was out of the bag.

The following day, Iranian Majil (Parliament) Speaker Rafsanjani admitted that the *Al-Shiraa* article was indeed true and later held a press conference displaying the signed Bible as proof. The White House initially denied that the story was true, although press sources confirmed its accuracy. As the reporters continued to question Reagan about the secret arms deals with Iran, recently released hostage David Jacobsen berated the press by saying "In the name of God, would you please just be responsible and back off?" But the press didn't back off.

Less than two weeks after the *Al-Shiraa* article first ran, Reagan was forced to respond. On national television, he addressed the American people, saying, "For 18 months now, we have had underway a secret diplomatic initiative in Iran. The initiative was undertaken for the simplest and best reasons: to renew a relationship with Iran; to bring an honorable end to the bloody six-year war between Iran and Iraq; to eliminate state-sponsored terrorism and subversion, and to affect the safe return of all hostages." Possibly, by mentioning the hostages last, President Reagan was hoping that the American people would believe that the release of the American hostages was the primary reason for the arms deals. If this was his plan, it did not work.

Furthermore, in Reagan's speech, he pleaded with the American people not to believe the rumors being spread throughout Washington by the press. President Ronald Reagan personally asked the American people to trust his version of the "facts." "During the course of our secret discussions, I authorized the transfer of small amounts of defensive weapons and spare parts for defensive systems to Iran...These modest deliveries, taken together, could easily fit into a single cargo plane...We did not—repeat—did not trade weapons or anything else for hostages, nor will we." A Los Angeles Times poll released a few days later says that 79% of Americans rejected Reagan's explanation of the Iranian arms deals.

As Reagan tried desperately to save his political reputation, he held another press conference on November 19, saying the arms shipments sent to Iran were "miniscule." President Reagan, known as the "Great Communicator," also stated four times that Israel had absolutely no involvement in the arms deals. A few minutes after the press conference, a correction was issued. "There may have been some misunderstandings of one of my answers tonight. There was a third country involved in our secret project with Iran." That country was Israel.

Events were quickly unfolding. On November 21, William Casey, director of the CIA, appeared before the House and Senate Intelligence Committees, looking into the CIA's role in the arms shipments. Colonel Oliver North was told that the Justice Department would inspect his files the next day. Almost instantly the shredding machine in North's office went into overdrive as evidence was destroyed. Sadly for North and *The Enterprise*, the shredder jammed. On November 22, a Justice Department official found an April 1986 memo in North's office that was addressed directly to President Reagan outlining the Iranian arms sales and the diversion of funds to the Contras. As part of the public show, Ed Meese, head of the Justice Department, asked North if his memo to Reagan was truthful. North confirmed its truth. Apparently President Reagan forgot about the April 1986 memo and had to be reminded by Meese. Reagan's supposed reaction was "horror," even though all signs say that he knew about and encouraged the actions, even specifically authorized some.

On November 25, 1986 Meese officially announced to the nation that arms were traded to Iran and the profits from the illegal arms sales were diverted to the Contras. President Reagan, at the same conference, said that he was "not fully informed on the nature of the activities" undertaken by his staff. Reagan then announced that Admiral Poindexter, the National Security Advisor to the President, had resigned and that Lieutenant Colonel Oliver North was fired earlier in the day.

In an interview with *Time* magazine a few days afterwards, President Reagan called the man he just fired for illegal activities a "national hero." Reagan went on to blame the press for "interfering with the release of more hostages." "There is bitter bile in my throat...This whole thing boils down to great irresponsibility on the part of the press." By this time, President Reagan was beginning to realize how deep a crisis he was in. In the first days after the scandal broke, he was reported to have had several long and rambling conversations with the king of Presidential scandals himself, Richard Nixon. In defense of his friend, Richard Nixon told reporters that it was "time to get off (Reagan's) back."

But President Reagan was finding few friends as 1986 was coming to a close. A long time ally and "rabid supporter," Congressman Robert Dornan, stunned the Reagans by refusing to defend the President over his role in Iran-Contra. In response, Dornan told reporters that when someone in his district asked if it was true that Reagan had given arms to people he thought were responsible for killing the Marines in Lebanon, he became perplexed. "It's hard to respond to that."

On December 9, 1986 Colonel North and Admiral Poindexter invoked their 5th Amendment rights and refused to testify further in front of the House Foreign Affairs Committee about their roles in the "Iran-Contra Scandal." North said "I don't think there is another person in America that wants to tell this story as much as I do." Soon North would have his chance. By this time, everyone involved was beginning to feel the heat—especially William Casey. Casey, the man believed to have initiated and masterminded the arms-for-hostages deals, was questioned by the House Select Committee on Intelligence (HSCI) for over four hours. As director of the Central Intelligence Agency, Casey could not seem to remember anything that happened concerning the arms-for-hostages deals or the diversion of funds.

After hours of saying "I don't know" to nearly every question asked of him, Casey reportedly had the congressional committee laughing at the sheer volume of information Casey supposedly had no knowledge of. The rapidly unfolding scandal then took an unexpected turn when Casey suddenly had a seizure in Washington office, putting an end to his further testimony on the matter.

The Interesting Death of William Casey

On December 15, the day before William Casey was to testify before the HSCI, a CIA physician visited Casey in his office. Supposedly, in the middle of the visit, Casey suffered a severe seizure and had to be rushed to Georgetown University Hospital. As a result, he was unable to appear before the HSCI and would never be forced to publicly account for any of his deeds.

After his examination at Georgetown, Casey's CIA doctor told him that he had a brain tumor that had to be operated on right away. Casey, a man who was well aware of what his agency was capable of doing, did not like the idea of having brain surgery performed on him at that crucial time. He asked if his doctor could use radio therapy instead of the invasive and potentially life-threatening surgery. However, his doctor, employed by the same agency that had carried out several coups and assassinations in its short history, insisted on the major surgery.

Two days later, a malignant tumor was removed from Casey's brain. Sadly for Casey, while the surgery removed the tumor, doctors also "accidentally" damaged the part of his brain that dealt with speech and left the director of the CIA incapacitated right before he was to testify to Congress. In his biography of William Casey, Joseph Persico said that one of the persistent rumors at the time was that "the CIA or the NSC or the White House had arranged to have a piece of the brain removed from the man who knew the secrets".

While some in this country may find it hard to believe that someone in the CIA would do such a thing, a citizen of Chile, Guatemala, or Iran might suggest that a simple look into the CIA's history would show otherwise. It was also later learned through Oliver North's testimony that William Casey had discussed the potential need for a "fall guy" if the truth of these dealings ever came to light. Did Casey become the fall guy? In any case, whether William Casey died of natural causes or was picked off by "spooks," the end result was the same and Casey never had another opportunity to speak to Congress concerning what he knew about his role in the scandal.

William Casey died on May 6, 1987.

The Contra Drug Ring

As more and more incredible stories began to leak out about the depths of this scandal, one persistent rumor about CIA/Contra drug smuggling took on a life of its own.

Since the early eighties, rumors had surfaced about the Nicaraguan Contras financing their war against the Sandinistas with money raised through the drug trade. It was alleged that the Contras had a drug smuggling network that brought cocaine into the U.S., most of it going to Los Angeles. While the CIA was never accused of actually participating, the cocaine smuggling ring was well-known within the Agency.

Furthermore, little was done to stop the smugglers as they were making money to fund the Contras. This becomes all the more incredible when contrasted with the

administrations heavily publicized "Just say No!" propaganda campaign against drugs. These damaging allegations first came to light as the Iran-Contra scandal was unfolding. Through Freedom of Information Act releases, it was learned that high-ups within the CIA were well aware of the drug trafficking, as was Ollie North and the White House. There was little consideration as to the devastating effects that the cocaine trade would have on the residents of Los Angeles, only to the profitability of the trade. Contra agents sold the drugs directly to both the Bloods and Crips street gangs.

To assist, the CIA and various departments within the DEA made certain that the trade would continue unimpeded. This allowed Los Angeles to be flooded with cocaine, giving rise to the crack epidemic and gang violence that soon spread throughout the country, all the while making substantial profit for the Contras. When allegations first surfaced, they were investigated by congress, but soon "forgotten." Almost a decade later the same allegations resurfaced when Gary Webb, a reporter for the San Jose Mercury News, wrote a series of articles entitled "The Dark Alliance" detailing the extent of the Contra drug trade in LA. The story caused a major sensation throughout the U.S., bringing both praise and criticism.

Eventually, *The San Jose Mercury News* backed away from the story, even though none of the major charges were ever refuted. The following year, the CIA's own internal investigation proved that Gary Webb's assertions were, in fact, true: members of the Contras were smuggling drugs into the U.S. with the CIA's knowledge, and possible encouragement. As for Webb, the vindication did little to help his career. He was essentially forced to quit the paper and had trouble finding another job at a major newspaper, despite multiple awards for "The Dark Alliance" stories. Sinking into depression, Webb, the reporter who had written some of the most damning articles in CIA history, committed suicide—supposedly—by shooting himself in the head. Not once, but twice.

The Joint Senate-House Iran-Contra Hearings

Early 1987 saw President Reagan's approval rating drop dramatically, as he was continuously dogged by the press over the Iran-Contra Scandal. A commission headed by Republican Senator John Tower had been set up to investigate the allegations. An independent council, Lawrence Walsh, was also appointed to investigate what the President knew or didn't know about the clandestine operation.

In February 1987, the Tower Commission completed its report. To many people's surprise, the report was heavily critical of the actions of Ollie North, John Poindexter, Secretary of Defense Caspar Weinberger, and a host of other participants. While it was expected to be light on President Reagan, the Tower Commission report surprised many in its criticism of President Reagan saying that if he did not know what was going on in his White House, he should have.

In the summer of 1987, select committees of the Senate and the House of Representatives held public hearings on the unfolding scandal. Broadcast on national television, the hearings mostly made heroes of the participants while doing little to probe the complex and somewhat more critical questions about the deals. Instead, the committees focused mostly on whether or not the President knew that profits generated by arms sales to the Iranians had been diverted to the Contras. Deeper subjects were almost completely ignored.

Little time was given during the lengthy questioning periods, much of which was broadcasted on live television, to the possibly more damning implications of the U.S. participation in the "Dirty War" in Central America. The ethics involved in selling arms to Iran to help them fight the Iraqis in a war that had already killed hundreds of thousands on both sides were also ignored.

Vice President George Bush's reported role in the scandal was barely discussed. Nor was the alleged CIA participation in drug smuggling to help fund the Contra war. More fundamentally important, little discussion was given to what it meant to live in a democracy where un-elected "secret governments" were directing and acting upon their own foreign policy, with little means of accountability, all the while supporting some of the most brutal dictatorships in the world. Instead, Colonel North, Admiral Poindexter, and Richard Secord were allowed to give what amounted to lengthy infomercials on why the U.S. should be supporting the Contras. Few critical questions came from either side of the aisle, and some Senators even went so far as to give their own pro-Contra speeches without acknowledging that *The Enterprise* had broken the very laws Congress itself had made.

Ollie North, who, as writer Paul Brancato described, "wore an expression like a wounded hound and spoke in a voice trembling with patriotism," was allowed to become a populist hero even as he publicly admitted to lying about most of his previous testimony. In fact, the lies were so deep that it became literally impossible for Congress or the American people to know for certain what happened in Reagan's White House. Wrapping themselves in the flag and right-wing causes while relaying their deep concern for the hostages in Lebanon, nearly everyone involved justified their lies as the price of a "just cause." Few in Congress or the mainstream media dared question whether or not any of the causes were indeed "just," or even asked such basic questions as where the money went and who exactly profited from these missions. That said, the hearing did give the American public a glimpse into the inner-workings of Reagan's White House and the "secret governments" acting on his wishes and intentions.

I DON'T REME
I DON'T REME
I DON'T REME
I DON'T REME
I DON'T REME
I DON'T REMEMB
I DON'T REMEMBE
I DON'T REMEMBER
I DON'T REMEMBER

But was that enough? Supposedly, much of the operation was done in secret to give the President of the U.S. the ability to plausibly deny he knew anything about the extent of the operation. While it certainly is possible that Reagan didn't know the minutia of every interaction between his underlings and their secret partners, it is maybe more disturbing to think that un-elected military and intelligence officers had initiated, directed, and acted upon their own ideologies with little regard for anyone or anything but the supposed righteousness of their own cause.

In its official report on the Iran-Contra scandal, Congress had to admit that even after hours, days, and months of testimony and countless enquiries, interrogations, and investigations, they most likely still did not know what really had happened. In a rather frank section of the report, Congress admitted "In light of the destruction of material evidence by Poindexter and North and the death of Casey, all of the facts may never be known. The Committees cannot even be sure whether they heard the whole truth or whether Casey's "fall guy" plan was carried out at public hearings. With Casey dead, the White House had the perfect fall guy.

As more time passed, it soon became very clear that both President Reagan and Vice-President Bush knew quite a bit about the entire operation as memos began to surface implicating everyone involved. Still, the Congress lacked the resolve to pursue further actions against the President or the Vice-President. Reagan was criticized for not knowing what was being done in his name and on his watch, but soon bounced back in the polls and much was forgiven.

As for Colonel North and *The Enterprise*, little was done to hold them accountable for their crimes. In March of 1988, North and Poindexter were both indicted on multiple charges related to their lying to Congress. North was eventually found guilty and convicted of three minor charges and forced to resign in disgrace from his beloved Marine Corps. Admiral Poindexter was also found guilty and convicted of several felony charges, including lying to Congress, conspiracy, obstruction of justice, and altering and destroying documents related to the Congressional enquiry.

Both men, however, had their convictions overturned on appeal shortly afterwards—claiming the trials and convictions violated their Fifth Amendment right against self-incrimination stemming from their previous testimony in front of Congress. Robert McFarlane attempted suicide in the aftermath of the Iran-Contra Scandal, claiming that he let his country down. He recovered and eventually pled guilty to 4 felony counts of withholding information to Congress. He received probation and a $200,000 fine. Caspar Weinberger, who claimed to have been initially opposed to the arms deals, was indicted by independent council Lawrence Walsh for his participation in the scandal. However, both "Cap" Weinberger and Robert McFarlane, possibly as a Christmas gift, were given Presidential pardons by then-President George Bush on December 24, 1992 for all crimes past and those that might be uncovered later, related to Iran-Contra. Several other key figures that were prosecuted for crimes relating to the scandal were also pardoned as part of the George Bush Sr. Xmas amnesty package.

Ironically the only person to do any jail time for crimes related to the Iran-Contra scandal was a former minister from Odon, Indiana. Odon is the hometown of Admiral John Poindexter. Bill Breeden, a pacifist who lived in a teepee in the woods with his wife and two children, discovered that the Odon government had decided to honor their hometown hero by renaming one of its streets "John Poindexter Street." A critic of U.S. foreign policy, Breeden was outraged at this "celebration of immoral behavior in government." In protest, Bill Breeden stole the street sign honoring Poindexter and held it ransom for $30 million dollars, the amount of money transferred to the Contras from the Iranian arms sales.

In *The People's History of the United States,* Howard Zinn wrote that for his crime, the Indiana Unitarian minister "was apprehended, put on trial, and spent a few days in jail. As it turned out, Bill Breeden was the only person to be imprisoned as a result of the Iran-Contra affair."

Aftermath

When all of the cash diversions and allegations of drug trafficking came to light (and were mostly confirmed by a CIA internal investigation), the Contras disbanded and reorganized under a different name. Not long after, a peace deal was reached between the Contras and Sandinistas with the help of the president of Costa Rica. For the most part, the war was over. Part of the agreement was that Nicaragua was to have internationally monitored free elections. This was nothing new to Nicaraguans since all their post-Samoza elections had been internationally monitored and declared fair by third parties.

In 1990, with the knowledge that the fighting could resume if the Sandinistas were to win the election, Nicaraguans saw the writing on the wall and voted to replace Daniel Ortega with Violetta Chamora, an opponent of the Marxist Sandinistas. Today, Nicaragua is one of the poorest countries in the hemisphere. In 2006, the Nicaraguan people elected Daniel Ortega (once again) against the wishes of the U.S.. Although threats were made that an Ortega election would hurt US/Nicaraguan relations, the people of Nicaragua decided to vote their conscience anyway. Bogged down in a war in Iraq, it is doubtful the U.S. will further involve itself in Nicaragua—at least militarily.

The Iran-Contra Scandal was a major blow to Ronald Reagan's credibility, as well as to the credibility of the U.S. concerning terrorism, the Middle East, the war on drugs, and human rights issues. It was this humiliation that forced the Administration to swing hard in the opposite direction in the Iran-Iraq War. From now on, if anyone were to get cakes and guns, it would not be Iran. The U.S. had officially remained neutral for most of the war. While privately arming the Iranians, the U.S. sold the Iraqis mustard and nerve gas, which they used against the Iranian military. Playing both sides in this bloody war suited the U.S. government fine, but after revelations that Reagan had been sending Iran missiles privately while publicly calling them an enemy of America, the President needed a quick reversal in policy as part of his damage control efforts.

Almost immediately, the U.S. began to back Iraq. The U.S. went so far as to re-flag foreign merchant ships in the Persian Gulf that were headed to Iraq officially under the "stars and stripes." This would make any attacks on them an act of war against the U.S. according to (a twisting of) international law, thus ensuring that Iraq would continue to have an almost unimpeded flow of goods through its port cities. The support was so strong for Iraq, or—maybe closer to the truth—anti-Iran at any cost, that when Iraqi jets attacked the USS Stark Navy ship in the Persian Gulf killing dozens of American sailors, the U.S. did nothing in response.

Then, when Saddam Hussein gassed the Kurds (a crime that caused considerable uproar in the late 90s and prior to the U.S. invasion of Iraq in 2003, but little concern at the time) the reaction was not condemnation, but approval. Bob Dole was sent as a secret emissary to tell Saddam that the U.S. government had no problems with his use of chemical weapons.

As the war stepped up to new levels, the U.S. military began to take on an antagonistic role in the Persian Gulf in hopes of baiting the Iranians into an attack. The USS Vincennes, a guided missile cruiser, was on such a patrol on July 3, 1988 when it illegally entered Iranian waters chasing a small gunboat. In the confusion, the crew mistook Iranian Air Flight 655, a civilian commercial flight flying from Tehran to Dubai with 290 civilians aboard, for an Iranian F-14. The civilian airliner was shot down, killing all aboard. When asked if the U.S. would apologize to Iran for the massacre, Vice

President George Bush said "I will never apologize for the U.S. of America! I don't care what the facts are."

In his book *The Longest War*, Dilip Hiro asserts that this was one of the main reasons that the Ayatollah eventually accepted Saddam Hussein's proposal to end the war. Ayatollah Khomeini felt that if the U.S. could so brazenly strike down an Iranian civilian airliner with virtually no consequences (not to mention Hussein's continuous use of chemical weapons on Iran, much of which acquired through American channels), and that Hussein had the complete backing of the U.S. since the secret deals with Iran had come to light, then little would be gained by Iran from prolonging the bloodshed.

The Iranians and Iraqis reached a truce in August of 1988, ending the Iran-Iraq War. This put President Hussein in a favorable position with the U.S. While both sides declared victory in the 8-year war, Hussein reaped most of the benefits with his improved American relations. To some extent, Hussein felt he could do no wrong as far as the Americans were concerned. He had gotten away with an invasion of Iran, which the U.S. did not strongly disapprove of. He had the U.S. drop Iraq's status as a state sponsor of terrorism so it could purchase chemical weapons. It used mustard and nerve gas not only on the Iranian military, but also on the Iranian civilian populace as well as the Kurdish population.

The U.S. publicly condemned the actions, but privately continued favorable relations and a continuation of financial and military aid. This convinced Saddam Hussein that the U.S. would support him through good times and bad. Thus, when U.S. ambassador to Iraq April Glaspie was summoned to a meeting with Saddam Hussein and his Deputy Prime Minister, Tariq Aziz, she was told in so many words that Iraq was considering an invasion of Kuwait to stop them from taking potential oil revenue by "slant drilling" across the border. Hussein then asked Ambassador Glaspie what the U.S. reaction would be to a hypothetical invasion. Glaspie reassured him that the U.S. had "no opinion on inter-Arab disputes such as your border dispute with Kuwait." She furthermore went on to say the position would be reiterated by the Secretary of State. This, along with a letter from, then-President, George Bush three days later, expressing his keen interest on improving relations with Baghdad, helped to assure Hussein of his favorable status with the new administration and of U.S. neutrality after an invasion. This, of course, proved not to be the case.

On August 2, 1990 Saddam Hussein invaded Kuwait, beginning what would be called *The Gulf War*. It's important to note that if it were not for Ambassador Glaspie's "green light," Hussein most likely would not have invaded Kuwait. To do so otherwise would have been suicide—and it was. Operation Desert Shield/Desert Storm was launched, thus ending in a U.S. victory that led to the decade long sanctions and eventually to the second U.S. invasion of Iraq in 2003.The rest, as they say, is history.

The Cast:

Elliot Abrams: Assistant Secretary of State, solicited contributions from foreign governments to aid the Contras. Claimed aiding the Contras was part of the Reagan Administration's "human rights" policy. Plead guilty to two counts of withholding information from Congress, but later pardoned by George Bush.

William Buckley: CIA station chief in Beirut. Notorious womanizer. Thought to be a security risk by CIA. Kidnapped by Islamic fundamentalists in 1984; tortured and executed, shocking the intelligence community.

George Bush: Vice president under Reagan. Sat in and participated in key meetings discussing arms for hostages deals according to several memos, but still claimed ignorance. As president, one of his last acts was a blanket pardon for everyone involved in Iran-Contra scandal, past, present, and future.

Adolfo Calero: Former CIA informant, manager of Coca-Cola's Managua branch, vocal in middle-class opposition to Somoza. Later recruited by CIA to lead and direct the Contras.

William Casey: Director of CIA under Reagan and chief architect of Contra War. Died after being stricken with a seizure the day before he was to testify before Congress. He went to the grave with his secrets.

Manucher Ghorbanifar: Iranian expatriate arms dealer and notorious liar. After failing several lie detector tests, CIA hired him to help arrange transfer of arms sales to Nicaraguan Contras. Oliver North stated that "Ghorba" gave him the idea in a men's room conversation.

Albert Hakim: Iranian expatriate and businessman who worked with defense contractors. Worked with Shah of Iran when he was in power, then worked with *The Enterprise* to help arrange arms sales to Iran. Convicted of defrauding the U.S. government.

Eugene Hasenfus: CIA pilot shot down in Nicaragua, exposing connection between CIA, Contras, and later Iranian arms sales. Was tried in Nicaragua and sentenced to 25 years in prison, but was pardoned by President Daniel Ortega. Later convicted of exposing himself in public on several occasions.

Robert McFarlane: Marine Lt Col, National Security Advisor under Ronald Reagan, and one of the original planners of the Contra war against Nicaragua. Plead guilty to four counts of withholding information from Congress, but later pardoned by George Bush.

Edwin Meese III: Reagan's embattled Attorney General. Delayed investigations in nearly all aspects of the scandal.

Oliver North: Marine Lt. Col., staff officer with the National Security Council (NSC), Vietnam war veteran, and fervent anti-communist. A strong supporter of Contras and key planner of Arms-for-Hostage trade with Iran. He was convicted of defrauding the U.S. government, but later pardoned by George Bush.

Daniel Ortega: Leader of Sandinstas and president of Nicaragua. Main target of U.S. anti-communist propaganda campaign. In 1990, was voted out of office. In 2006, was elected to the presidency again where he is currently serving the people of Nicaragua.

John Poindexter: Navy Admiral who served as Reagan's National Security Advisor. Helped plan and execute arms for hostages trade and transfer of funds to Nicaraguan Contras, while allegedly leaving Reagan out of conversations to give him "plausible deniability." Convicted of defrauding the U.S. Government, but later pardoned by George Bush.

Ronald Reagan: President who called Iran's leaders "the strangest collection of loony tunes and squalid criminals since the Third Reich," whose administration later sold arms to these same leaders. Focused early on the Contras in Nicaragua. Pursued a U.S. foreign policy supporting ongoing wars in Guatemala, El Salvador, and Honduras. Claimed ignorance of all illegal actions. Never convicted.

Richard Secord: Air Force Major General, air-wing commander for the CIA's operations in Laos. Key member of NSC who helped arrange arms trade with Iran for hostages. Convicted of defrauding U.S. government, but later pardoned by George Bush.

Anastasio Somoza: Dictator of Nicaragua, overthrown in Sandanista revolution of 1979. Fled country, stealing most of the money in Nicaragua's national treasury in the process. Assassinated in Paraguay a year later.

Caspar Weinberger: Reagan's Secretary of Defense and former director of Bechtel Corporation. Supposedly raised objections to the trading of weapons for hostages, but did little to stop this program. As Secretary of Defense, ensured war with Nicaragua would continue by any means necessary. He was charged with two counts of lying to Congress, but was pardoned in mid-trial.

Sources / Recommended Reading:

The Iran-Contra Scandal; The Declassified History. Edited by Peter Kornbluh and Malcolm Byrne.
A Very Thin Line; The Iran-Contra Affairs. Theodore Fraper. Touchstone, Simon, and Schuster
Witness, Mansur Rafizadeh.
Iran-Contra Affair (Abridged Edition), (Congressional Report) New York Times Books
The Longest War, Dilip Hiro
Saddam Hussein, Efraim Karsh and Inari Rautsi
The Clothes Have No Emperor, Paul Slanksy
October Surprise, Gary Sick
The Dark Alliance, Gary Webb
The Tower Commission Report, New York Times Books
Pity the Nation, Robert Fisk